The Librarian Speaking

Interviews with University Librarians

The Librarian Speaking

Interviews with University Librarians

By

GUY R. LYLE

UNIVERSITY OF GEORGIA PRESS
ATHENS

Contents

Preface

"A generation ago," says Professor F. E. L. Priestley of the University of Toronto, "university librarians were usually academics themselves, running the library on something like an amateur basis, not always with a high degree of efficiency, but with precisely the same conception of the librarian's function and status as their academic fellows." With students and faculties increasing and libraries accumulating collections of increasing size and complexity, the burden of providing adequate library service required something more than the casual attention of an academic such as a professor of English or the classics. Just when the change took place from the scholar and amateur librarian to the new type of professional bookman-librarian is anybody's guess, but I would place it well into the 1920's, when the boom in college enrollments and curricula precipitated a revolution in library use and a need for more systematic and orderly methods of organization and reader assistance. At that time, the library became identified as the workshop of the social sciences and the humanities. The new professional bookman-librarian bent his energies in the direction of efficiency and utility. He established reserve reading rooms, opened the book stacks, encouraged reference service, formulated programs for instruction in the use of the library, brought departmental libraries under some measure of control, provided a centralized catalog to all library resources, founded browsing and dormitory libraries, and encouraged the college or university president to think in terms of larger and better book programs. His approach was businesslike, pragmatic; he exploited every possible angle of library service that looked promising to the support of instruction and research.

The conviction or suspicion that university librarianship is once again reaching a turning point in its history is widespread in the world of librarianship. At the moment technology is one of the compelling forces constantly shaping librarianship. At the same time specialization proliferates. The library is viewed as one element in a complex communication system and the pressure is on librarians to produce faster and better ways of acquiring, organizing, and retrieving information if the library is to make its best contribution. The description of what the new era in librarianship will bring is not simple to forecast nor can it be clearly predicted at this time, but the symptoms are there. One need only open one's eyes and ears. It will take some time for the technological yearning and learning that is being churned up in the library journals, library institutes, and library conventions to change into action. When this happens, library aims and services will probably be altered to a degree which will make them unrecognizable to those who have helped to make university librarianship what it is today.

Both continuity and change are essential elements of librarianship. Obviously, there is no such thing as an overnight revolution in library methods. Where there is major change, there is usually an extended period of transition. The 1960's would appear to be the middle ground between the basic values which have made university librarianship what it is today and the planning for the technological changes of tomorrow. I wish that it were possible to make an intelligible presentation of librarianship in this period of transition, but by any indication that I can see this is still impossible. No veteran librarian is without his partisan preconceptions; few have the knowledge to fully comprehend the revolution of the future. Instead, what I have to offer in this book is an informal exploration of some of the persistent and critical problems of university librarianship in the United States in the 1960's by some of the leading librarians of today. It is an attempt, however, to present librarianship in human terms, not as a series of descriptions of past techniques or as a catalog of the latest developments resulting from the application of technology to librarianship. It is a distillation of the experience of these librarians on matters which I thought were of special interest to them or about which they knew more than most. If any justification were necessary to give voice to their opinions, one might add that it is highly desirable to take a look at where university librarianship now stands while it is still possible to grasp the field as a whole and before it becomes fragmented into a rapidly expanding complex of knowledge communication.

The technique of questions and answers has its limitations but it makes for stimulating and pleasant reading. Perhaps for this reason, it may be hoped that the talks will appeal not only to librarians but to those who are engaged in educational practice or deeply interested in education. Because public relations has not shed its radiance over college and university librarians, the general public knows very little of librarians; the usual stereotype confounds the senses and hides the flesh-and-blood person. Perhaps these interviews will provide an antidote. The interview technique may also be one way to help make a more intelligible presentation of library aims to administrators, faculty, and others engaged in roles affecting university librarianship.

The selection of persons interviewed is purely arbitrary and needs no explanation. I brooded some over the questions, but the replies were spontaneous and unrehearsed. Each person interviewed was given the opportunity to look over the transcript in case he wished to extend or recast his replies so as to afford a more accurate representation of his point of view. Minimal editing was done by the editor since this is a form of oral history and there can be significance in the way a librarian expressed his views.

It remains only to express my deep appreciation to the men and women who responded so generously to my request for the interviews. I am, as always, under great obligation to my wife for typing, reading proof, and for many helpful suggestions.

Guy R. Lyle

Emory University Library
Atlanta, Georgia

Kenneth J. Brough

KENNETH BROUGH (rhymes with *crow*) is a most attractive man, slightly old-fashioned in an English professorial way but very much the modern university librarian. He has a penetrating and sinewy mind and his talk is salted with homely wit and irony. One has the feeling that here is a man of great intellectual integrity and force. One of his former student employees said of him: "the atmosphere was always pleasant in the library and you could talk to him at any time. Personal relations were generally on the formal side but there were frequent staff meetings and discussions and Dr. Brough's good humor never failed him."

Originally intending to be a high school teacher and principal, he turned to librarianship in 1934 after seven years in the school system and became librarian of Eastern New Mexico University. Prior to settling down to librarianship in earnest, however, he occupied himself with a three-year stint with the U.S. Army and earned a Ph.D. degree from Stanford University. His library training was done at Columbia University in 1942. In 1949 he came to his present position as librarian of San Francisco State College. His book *The Scholar's Workshop, Evolving Conceptions in Library Service* (1953), published by the University of Illinois Press, examined the historical evolution in the United States of many of the concepts which are regarded as fundamental in college and university library administration to-

1

day. Based on original documents, the book is an admirable blending of scholarship and readability.

The following interview took place at San Francisco State College on August 20, 1968.

Since coming to Berkeley, I have heard a good bit of talk about the use of budgetary formulas in determining library support in the state college libraries. Can you tell me something about these formulas, what they are, and how they came into being?

I think I can. Early in the 1950's the librarians of the California state colleges were trying to improve their library situation—salaries, working conditions, and the like. The college librarians organized to work together along this line and produced several reports aimed at justifying better support. These first reports were unsuccessful, but the activities related to them brought us into contact with officials in the State Department of Education who were able and willing to help us. We soon learned from these officials and from faculty committees working on budgetary problems in other areas that the approach most likely to be accepted by reviewing authorities would be a careful analysis of library operations expressed in a formula which could be used in budgeting for all the California state colleges. We changed our tactics accordingly and after months of hard work were able to recommend our first successful staffing formula.

Was this formula similar to the "work-load" formulas devised by the American Library Association classification and pay plans for academic libraries in the late 1940's?

In our earliest reports we used the ALA standards which you mention, but we found them to be unacceptable. In developing our staffing formula we itemized the tasks performed in our own libraries and insofar as feasible measured the time required to do these tasks. For example, how long does it take to acquire a book—to order, catalog, and get it on the shelf? We had a long and awkward formula when we assembled all our factors, but the approach was accepted. The State Department of Finance assigned an analyst to improve on our efforts, and the result was a staffing formula that bettered our situation substantially and that was relatively easy to apply.

Did this formula provide both professional and nonprofessional staff?

Both. It produced a total figure from which was derived a percentage for each of the professional, clerical, and student assistant staff groups.

Was a formula established to improve library salaries?

No. In working to improve salaries we used comparative data, the salaries paid in comparable institutions throughout the United States. This seems to be the most common approach in efforts to raise pay scales.

Has the original organization of librarians, who initiated the formula or organized approach to the development of the college libraries, continued to this day?

Before we got very far in our activities we discovered that we had to have a broader base of support than just librarians. We were fortunate in being able to get the help of a man in the State Department of Education by the name of Dr. Joel Burkman, who at that time was the Assistant Division Chief, State Colleges and Teacher Education. He was unusually able and was very influential with the presidents of the state colleges, who met in council and who served as a legislative body for the system. Through Dr. Burkman's efforts we had a committee appointed, a committee on organization and salaries of state college library staffs. The chairman of the committee was H. E. Brakebill, then the business manager of San Francisco State College and now vice chancellor for business affairs of the California state colleges. Our president at that time, Dr. J. Paul Leonard, was interested in our efforts and apparently encouraged the business manager to devote some time to this project.

Who served with the business manager on the committee?

Dr. Burkman was closely associated with the committee; he always met with us as an adviser. There were two college librarians—Dr. Henry Madden of Fresno and myself—the business manager from Fresno, and one of the deans from San Jose, as I recall it now. The membership varied somewhat from year to year. I remember that another college librarian, Joyce Backus of San Jose, met with us most of the time. The committee met fairly frequently, maybe as many as three or four meetings a year for about ten years. Originally we were formed to work on the classification and pay plan, but we found it important and expedient to make recommendations on related matters as we went along, such as the expansion of the book collections. The committee was disbanded in 1960 in a general reorganization of the committee system of the California state colleges. A few years later, when control of the state colleges had shifted from the State Department of Education to an independent Board of Trustees, a new committee on library development was appointed. Dr. Glenn Dumke, the chancellor, had been keenly interested in library problems when president of San Francisco State College in 1957-1961, and he was most influential in bringing library matters to the attention of the trustees soon after their organization.

Has the new committee been effective in securing library support?

The principal contribution of the committee on library development has been to improve sharply the level of support for the acquisition of books and other materials. The fiscal authorities have accepted a plan to bring the book collections of all the California state colleges to a level of forty volumes per student by 1973-1974. Forty volumes per student was approximately the median figure in college and university libraries throughout the United States when the committee made its first report. This may seem to be a modest plan, but it has brought about very substantial growth for our collections. The plan has been specially beneficial to our newly established institutions because budgetary allocations have been based primarily on enrollment expected in 1973-1974 rather than on the comparatively small enrollments of their first years of operation.

Well, that is a very brief review of the use of formulas in improving the level of support for the libraries of the California state colleges. It seems to me that our experience clearly demonstrates the importance of cooperative and systematic effort.

There is another matter of growing concern to librarians— the question of unions. Since you have had first-hand experience, will you tell me something of the history of your student library assistant union problem?

As I remember it, we first heard of the student assistant union about mid-year 1966-1967. Some students called on me and said they wanted to form a union of the student employees in the library. I talked to them. I wasn't hostile. They had some backing from the student newspaper; the editor would publish an article every week or so about the student employees in the library forming a union. During this year they did not make much progress; we had some interesting conversations and that was about the size of it.

The following year—this would be in the fall of 1967-1968—a different group of students made an appointment to meet with me. As I recall there were four or five of them and we met here in our office. They had elected a young woman to be their spokesman. After introductions she straightened up and said abruptly, "We have formed this student employees union and these are our demands!" Then she read a list of the things they were demanding. At first I was a bit resentful because of the manner of approach and because of the implication that we had a very undesirable work situation for student assistants in our library. I remember expressing the idea that it didn't take a union to get into my office to talk about problems. We kept the conversation friendly, nevertheless, and I tried to get a clear understanding of what they were after. They wanted better pay, and that was easy to grasp because our rate of pay was low for the time and place. There was great concern about grievances, also, and about the machinery for handling grievances. At first this surprised me because I had no evidence to indicate that student assistants were mistreated by supervisors. As a matter of fact, as you know, student assistants are generally treated rather liberally. We organize their work schedules to suit their class programs, make all sorts of adjustments, and so forth. In the discussion it developed that the grievances which the students had in mind related almost entirely to pay. We have several different rates of pay, and in some cases, according to their opinion, a student on one side of the building may have been getting $1.50 an hour while another student on the other side of the building—perhaps doing about the same thing but classified differently—would be getting $1.70.

Basically then their grievances had to do with a low wage scale and with a differential in pay among student employees?

These matters were certainly important, but there is more to it. It is more than just having a favorable work situation; they want to be the ones who have brought it about. In other words, instead of just having a situation where there is fair consideration and fair play, they want to have fair play because they insisted on it and got it. They want to be recognized as a voice in the administration. I have had the feeling that some of them are practicing to be labor organizers after college. Parenthetically, about a year before I heard anything about a union of library employees, the students who work in our college cafeteria had successfully formed a union. They were able to do this—to gain recognition and to get a contract—because they are not paid by the state. They are paid by the foundation set up to manage the food service and to operate the bookstore. At the outset they were able to get their pay up to $1.90 per hour with improved fringe benefits, and later their pay was advanced to $2.25 per hour.

Is this group affiliated with the federation of municipal employees which is signing up clerical employees on the campuses in the Bay area?

I think they have some alliance but I do not remember what it is. At least they have a union and a closed shop and they have a contract. A contract is what the student library assistants want, of course. In our later discussions it has become quite clear that recognition as the sole bargaining agent for student employees in the library is the objective most important to them. Moreover, they want a contract guaranteeing this status and they want the expiration date of the contract to coincide with the expiration date of the contract held by the cafeteria employees. Such an arrangement would obviously facilitate cooperation between the two unions and would increase their strike power. Although the library has not entered into any contract—and so far as I am aware we are in no position to do so—we have developed a manual of information which outlines working conditions, pay, grievance procedures, and the like. In preparing this manual we have had the help of the college personnel officer and we have sought the suggestions of student employees. Reaction of the students to the manual has been very lukewarm, however; they do not accept it as a substitute for a contract.

Are there contracts for custodial help?

No contract, so far as I know, but some of the custodians are members of a union. A representative of the union comes to the campus to assist employee members in grievance negotiations and the like. Members of the union are not permitted to strike because it is held to be illegal for state employees to strike.

Am I correct in thinking that you pay your student help from state funds?

Yes, but that did not keep them from striking! Whether or not it was a legal strike is another question. The strike occurred toward the end of the spring semester after a series of conferences with union representatives which ended in disagreement on most points.

Did they walk off the job?

Not all, but about half of them did, according to our estimate. Our information was incomplete: we did not know how many students were members of the union and we could not always be sure that absence from the job was due to strike activities rather than to illness or other personal circumstances. We were able to maintain service fairly well by employing nonstriking students for additional hours and by temporarily assigning full-time clerical workers to some of the tasks commonly done by student assistants. After three days the strike fizzled out. The strikers were losing money, and they couldn't afford to lose much money. Some of them probably got tired of parading outside with placards. We took back everyone who wanted to work and there weren't any punitive measures. Then we began to negotiate toward better agreement in the future but without great success. In their last effort of the school year, union representatives still held to recognition as sole bargaining agent with appropriate contract as the essential requirement, and the library was unable and unwilling to go into such an arrangement. So we have yet to find a way of working together that will satisfy all parties—not a contract unless we have some fundamental changes, but some means of providing for student employees greater participation in working out the terms and conditions of their employment as student assistants.

What benefits have they secured?

We were paying from $1.50 up to $2.00 per hour. In this current year we are starting with $1.70 and paying up to $2.00. What we did was to raise the beginning pay, which meant an increase in our overall cost per hour of about 8 percent. A 5 percent increase in state allocations for student assistant pay covered most of our increase. The balance was made possible by reducing the total number of hours of student employment in the library.

Another benefit is the provision of a lounge for student assistants. At first we thought that we could meet the demand for this facility by arranging for students to use the existing staff lounge, but the librarians and clerks were against it because of the limited space. The lounge has only about 500 square feet to care for 75 full-time employees, and they felt there was not room enough to accommodate more than 200 student assistants in addition. As matters worked out, we were able to convert 500 square feet in another attractive location. I'll show it to you because it may be the best lounge for student library employees in the world—who knows? At any rate, the students got the lounge and a raise in pay, and we expect to continue discussions without any unfriendliness. Although we may never reach complete agreement, we should be able to improve relationships and conditions steadily by cooperative effort.

Is your student rate of pay below the campus rate?

No. One thing we moved toward strongly last year was to get a campus-wide pay scale, and we were successful.

Are students involved with the library in any other way administratively or in an advisory capacity? Do you have a student representative on the faculty library committee?

We have a faculty committee called the committee on instructional materials, which deals with problems that arise in connection with the library or with the audiovisual center. A student is appointed to this committee by the president of the student body, and this is the case with the other faculty committees. Beyond this, and as a result of the union of student assistants in the library, we now have an arrangement whereby two student employees attend meetings of the library staff. One of these students is a member of the union, and the other is not a member.

Are these meetings of the library staff sponsored by a professional staff association?

Our librarians are not formally organized in a staff association, but we have monthly meetings of the staff except during the summer. All librarians are eligible to attend except those scheduled for minimal staffing. Subprofessional and clerical employees are included in one meeting each semester. No one is required to attend, of course.

What do you find to discuss at monthly meetings?

We consider staff welfare matters and policies and procedures in connection with the operation of the library. We have an agenda committee composed of elected members, one from the Librarian I and II classes, one from one of the upper grades of librarians, and one from the clerical staff. I serve as an *ex officio* member. The agenda committee is a communications device that grew out of our experience over the years. It became evident, as we went along, that some members of the staff were reluctant for one reason or another to introduce topics in open meeting. They might feel strongly about certain matters but would not find it easy to speak up. The agenda committee provides opportunity for private communication. A suggestion box might accomplish the same purpose, to a certain extent, but the committee is better because the members actively seek out the topics of greatest concern to the staff. The committee meets once a month shortly before the staff meeting and considers all matters brought before it, disposing of everything in one way or another. Simple matters which require only administrative action are usually handled directly. For example, if someone has suggested that paper cups be made available in the staff lounge it may seem best just to ask the storekeeper to provide them. When the agenda committee was newly established we felt a compunction to bring up all topics in staff meeting. As a result we had a few meetings where we talked about such ridiculous minutiae that everyone was bored, so now we skim off the trivia and include on the agenda only the more important matters. But any topic which appears to involve an issue is brought up for discussion in the staff meeting.

How are the subjects on the agenda presented at the meeting?

When we prepare the agenda we may agree that a member of our committee should open the discussion by presenting the background and the principal issues, or we may decide to ask another member of the staff to do so. Or it may be that the person suggesting the topic for consideration has agreed to introduce it. I sometimes volunteer when I believe that I have some special information about the topic.

Then you feel that these meetings have been useful to the staff as well as to you?

Oh yes, I do. We keep our lines of communication open. Instead of having the administration in one compartment and a staff association in another, we are all in the same boat. We also have another series of meetings not yet mentioned here—the department heads meet once a month. At these meetings we try to deal with major policy matters. It is our experience that we make much more progress if the group discussing such matters is experienced and has thorough knowledge of our library. At one time we were initiating such questions in the general staff meetings and were wasting an awful lot of time. In many cases, the less experienced staff members did not really have a grasp of the factors involved, and frequently we got hung up on minor points. The minutes of meetings of the department heads are sent to all librarians, and opportunity for questions and further discussion about the topics considered is made in general staff meetings.

Are there opportunities for staff members to exchange views on personnel matters with their colleagues in other academic libraries?

Until recent years the chief librarians of the state colleges were the only group that could get together with any regularity. As a result, we usually took the lead in efforts to get salaries raised and to improve welfare conditions generally for the librarians in the California state colleges. Four or five years ago, however, the librarians were successful in forming a Round Table (now a Division) of the California Library Association, and this action has made it possible to bring together at the annual conference of the association a sizable number of librarians of all grades from all the state college campuses. It is possible to pay the expenses of delegates attending these annual meetings. This new state-wide organization has brought on a new group of leaders; it has given all our librarians, regardless of grade, opportunities to assume leadership if they are ready for it and if they want it. As a result, this organization has taken over the main struggle for status, for better salaries, and for better working conditions.

How and to whom does this organization present its recommendations?

As resolutions formally transmitted to the Council of the California Library Association. Endorsement by the Council and by the Executive Board is very important. Delegates also report to their local memberships, who in turn usually seek further support through their representation in local academic senates and chapters of the Association of State College Professors, the American Association of University Professors, the American Federation of Teachers, and the California State Employees Association. Vigorous efforts are made to secure the endorsement of these organizations and to have the recommendations forwarded for review to the state-wide academic senate and to the state-wide organizations of the other groups.

Let me turn to something more personal. Was your book The Scholar's Workshop *a reworking of your dissertation?*

Yes. My dissertation was written under the direction of Professor W. H. Cowley of Stanford. His students regard him as a very special person, a fine scholar devoted to his teaching. He helped me immeasurably, and I feel that his encouragement and guidance were largely responsible for my book.

Well, it is certainly a fine book, one which is highly regarded in the library profession. No one can truly understand modern college librarianship without knowing something about the forces which led up to our present responsibilities. Likewise the librarians and their libraries are inseparable. Can you give me a brief summary of how you came into the library field?

I started out as a high school teacher. I came out of a small town where you didn't have much of a horizon. High school teaching and being a principal seemed a good way to go. And I liked teaching in high school, too, but it soon became apparent that I wasn't going to be able to continue because the pay was poor and the chances for advancement were limited. Then I decided that I would try to be a principal. The North Central Association required a master's degree in education, so I got a master's degree in education. After seven years in high school teaching, I accepted a position in a newly established junior college, with assignment half-time to teaching and half-time to developing the library. On a sort of an extracurricular basis, I had been librarian in the high school also. Even before that I was librarian of my Sunday School when I was a youngster. These little things may have had some influence on my career choice. The president of the junior college tried to create me in the image of B. Lamar Johnson,* so I was made half-time dean and half-time librarian. Well, it worked pretty well as long as we were small.

It worked pretty well for B. Lamar too, didn't it?

As a stepping-stone, it surely did. At any rate, I got to the point where the war caught me. After I got out, I had this wonderful GI opportunity; so I went to Stanford. I wanted to go to Stanford because I had gone there before for a semester in order to make my deanship at the junior college half-way respectable. I wanted to live out here on the west coast, too. I didn't want to go back to Chicago; so I worked out an arrangement to get my degree in education at Stanford while writing my dissertation on a library subject. I spent a semester at Berkeley getting the library school there to help me get started on a dissertation. This was accepted in lieu of a minor. That's the story. It was a sort of custom-made job, you know, a little different, but I have not regretted it. Librarianship has worked out very well for me. Someone has said if a man's life is not full of big things, it is full of little things. I have had my share of both.

---

*At this time Dr. Johnson held a rather unique position as librarian and
    Dean of Instruction at Stephens College.

William S. Dix

THE phenomenon of the Virginia gentleman who made his way via Rice University, Texas, to the Ivy is a cherished and permanent feature of the Southern university landscape. William Shepherd Dix was born in Winchester, Virginia, in 1910, and received his B.A. and M.A. from the University of Virginia. Continuing his studies in English language and literature at the University of Chicago, he received the Ph.D. in 1946. Before entering the field of librarianship, he taught English at Western Reserve, Williams College, and Harvard, and served Rice as librarian and professor of English prior to assuming the duties of University Librarian of Princeton in 1953.

Described by one of his associates as "amazingly fresh in his point of view," it is not surprising that Dr. Dix has been widely sought after by the library profession, foundations, and government for advice and assistance on boards and committees. A leader of the ALA's international relations and intellectual freedoms committees, he has also served as chairman of the Association of Research Libraries, and as one of the principal architects of the Shared Cataloging project of the Association of Research Libraries and the Library of Congress. His extracurricular activities include membership on the board of directors of the Council on Library Resources and on the advisory committees of the New Jersey State Library, Rutgers Library School, and Harvard and Duke University libraries.

From 1955 to 1961 he was a member of the United States National Commission for UNESCO, chairman for 1959 to 1961, and served as United States delegate to conferences in Paris and Manila. In the summer of 1969, he was elected president of the ALA.

Not the least of Dr. Dix's services to his profession is his talent for explaining a profession which needs all the explanation it can get. One such article, one of his best, appeared under the title "New Challenges to University Libraries" (*University: A Princeton Quarterly*, Fall, 1965).

If a man's success in librarianship is to be judged by the distinction of the positions he has held, by his contributions to his profession and to education in the broader sense, and by the duration of his pre-eminence, William Dix is without any doubt one of two or three of the most successful librarian-statesmen of the current decade.

The following interview took place at Princeton, June 18, 1969.

When I last visited Princeton I saw the Julian Street Library in Wilcox Hall and was much impressed by it as a good working collection for undergraduate students. I think you had around 5,000 volumes at the time and had in mind something like 10,000 volumes as an upper limit. Have you managed to keep within these limits, or have you found it desirable to expand?

We are very closely on schedule. The library now numbers a little less than its capacity of 10,000. We originally planned to add 200 volumes a year after we reached the capacity of the library, and to withdraw as many books as were added each year. It is not a static collection. We believe that withdrawals, substitutions, and additions, within the limit of 10,000 volumes, will keep it closely related to student needs and interests. These figures were arbitrary, of course, but we are running fairly close to schedule. There is a student committee on the library. We try to do everything the student wants and, by and large, I think we have done so. The committee's demands have not been unreasonable; they have tended to reflect current undergraduate interests. I think the library has been highly successful.

Does the Julian Street Library relieve the central library of a substantial portion of undergraduate library service?

Not large in any measurable sense because you may remember that this library, by definition, serves only the residents in a specific geographical area of the campus, a dormitory grouping. It was never intended to be the only one on the campus or to be an undergraduate library in the conventional sense at all. The ground rules are that anyone who happens to be in that part of the campus and wants to use it may do so. Only those who are identified as belonging in a specific residential area are permitted to borrow books. It is a little difficult to say how much of the load on Firestone is relieved. We have sufficient data on circulation, however, to suggest that the borrowing rate of the Julian Street Library is greater than any other part of the library system, excluding, of course, reserve book circulation. Very roughly, the circulation has been 5,000 out of 10,000 volumes a year, which is considerably higher than our university library circulation use as a whole. We have about two million printed books and an annual circulation of roughly half a million volumes. In other words, one in four as against the Julian Street Library circulation of one in two.

What proportion of the undergraduate student body is served by the Julian Street Library?

Roughly one-tenth. The circulation figures I gave you do not include within-the-library use, which is heavy, of course, in this kind of dormitory library.

Does the Julian Street Library siphon off many students who would otherwise be using Firestone as a study hall?

Well again, not substantially. Remember it has less than one hundred study seats. It is open from noon until midnight, whereas the central library is open from early in the morning until midnight. I look on this library mainly as a pedagogical thing. It has added to a residential part of the campus an intellectual element that would not exist without it. It is located in what one would call in our context a small student union building, which houses recreational activities, dining facilities, and social activities for this group of students. It has been successful to the extent that we are now actively planning another library in another dormitory complex, not a new set of buildings but an adjustment involving existing buildings.

When you first established the Julian Street Library you adopted certain judgments regarding the exclusion of paperbacks, back files of journals, sets of books, and so forth. Have you held to these judgments ·by and large?

I think so. No journal files, textbooks and paperbacks only when they are the best form in which to secure a text. We have not avoided the quality paperbacks arbitrarily. Literary sets are excluded unless demanded by a professor. For works in a foreign language the best translations are shelved beside the original texts. In most areas there has been an avoidance of highly specialized monographs. The reference collection is kept relatively small.

In your initial selection of titles for the Julian Street Library you made use of Harvard's Quincy House shelflist. I suppose you decided that Quincy House was nearest to what you had in mind for the Julian Street Library. I believe you then asked your faculty to go over the Quincy list title by title and to make their selections for your new library. Did they take this assignment conscientiously?

Yes, by and large, very conscientiously. In several cases, besides accepting inclusions and marking exclusions, they made lists of their own substituting for titles on the Quincy House lists. Perhaps the technique was a contributing factor. Some members of the faculty did not think too highly of the Quincy House list. They reacted to it and this stimulated them to do better. If we had simply said to Professor X that we would like him to suggest so many books in his field for this purpose, I doubt if the response would have been as good. I think it is good to give them something to shoot at. Now this was by no means the extent of compilation and editing. We accepted and rejected faculty suggestions; mostly accepted them, of course. As you no doubt remember, Mr. Kuhn undertook the task of editing the lists as a group. We added many titles, eliminated inequalities, and tried to provide a well-rounded, unified collection for the under-graduates.

One reason I asked this question is that I have seen critical reviews of the Street list. Are such criticisms perhaps a misin-

terpretation of the purpose and bounds prescribed for the collection?

I think so. It was never intended as a universal list. I saw one review, for example, which criticized the fact that we had included a set of the books written by Julian Street. Most of these probably would not have appeared in any 10,000 volume student library collection. It seemed to me a totally illegitimate criticism of this particular list. Our collection was named the Julian Street Library, and it seemed appropriate. This was a list geared to a particular situation, and, to some extent—to the extent that it serves the curriculum—to a particular curriculum. It was not intended to be a list of the 10,000 best books for undergraduates. It may have been a mistake to permit Bowker to publish it. Inevitably it got billed as an ideal selective undergraduate collection.

In spite of the critics and because of its high degree of selectivity, it has merit as a selection tool, has it not?

Well, in spite of what I've just said, I think it has been useful in the same way that the Quincy House list was useful to us. It is a starting point. It seems to me that when you are trying to accumulate a list of 10,000 volumes you start somewhere; you don't start in a vacuum. Regardless of the particular strength or weakness of a particular list, it is useful for this purpose. One thing emerged from the sale figures, at least, so I have been told. There was a considerable demand for something shorter than the traditional Shaw* type list. There is a gap here which the Julian Street list seemed to fill. One other thing we tried to do with this list should be made clear. We were interested in stimulating student extracurricular reading. The selections are not always the solid, best books; they are slanted in favor of the kind of book which will appeal to students—the art book, for example, with lots of good art reproductions in it, popular books for the non-scientist in the hope of interesting the humanist in science, and the like.

I think one might assume from your recent article in University: A Princeton Quarterly *that you favor the storage library concept. In this same article you say that the economy*

---

*C. B. Shaw, comp., *A List of Books for College Libraries*, 2nd. ed. Chicago: American Library Association, 1931.

in storage lies in compact storage of one type or another. What type of compact storage do you recommend on the basis of your experience and experiments in compact storage at Princeton?

Let me preface my reply by two general observations. One, I intended to say in the article to which you refer, and I have forgotten how I phrased it, that I defended the storage library concept reluctantly. In other words, I still have the feeling that it is better not to fragment to this extent if one can avoid it, but on the other hand, just as there are certain situations in which what is now almost the traditional undergraduate library seems to me a good thing, so there are situations in which the storage library is also a good thing. Some ten years ago I tried to say that I didn't think the concept of the separate undergraduate library should become library dogma. Since then I have been quoted widely in the literature as being opposed to the separate under-graduate library. Just recently I was in Japan and found myself addressed by a Japanese librarian in these words: "Oh, you're in this group; you oppose the splitting off of the undergraduate library." This is not true, of course; it all depends on the local situation. I have the same feeling about the storage library. It is not the best solution in every case. The second general ob-servation I wish to make relates to what you say I wrote about the economy factor in storage libraries. This may or may not be true. Ralph Ellsworth, as you may know, has just completed some studies on this question. I have seen only a partial draft of what he is getting ready to publish. He may suggest that there really is no economy if one considers all the costs.

With these two observations as premise, I will defend what we have just done at Princeton, which, I believe, appears to be working very well. We have a separate storage library building in a remote part of the campus, a low land-use area, that will house about 400,000 volumes. We are in process now of selecting carefully and slowly seldom-used volumes to be placed in this storage area. It seems to be working well and to be generally accepted by the campus community as a reasonable solution to our problem, and I repeat *our problem*. Our problem is that in the area where the central library is located, it is very difficult to see enough expansion over the next thirty or forty years to accommodate all the books which we will acquire. We are now in the process of expanding the central library building, but as

I look ahead I see this safety-valve factor an important one in gaining space for us.

Did you achieve the economy in construction you hoped for?

Our building has the simplest and most inexpensive type of warehouse shelving you can find—adjustable shelves—but we do not intend to adjust them simply because they come in units. I told the architects that if there is any glory in this for anybody it would be that we had been able to shelve a book at a lower cost per volume than anyone else. I'm afraid we haven't. Architecture ran away with us a little bit; the outside of the building is faced in brick, for example. I don't know that it needed to be, but the general requirements of that part of the campus seemed to suggest this for aesthetic reasons. So our cost may not be as low as one might like.

Do you recommend any particular type of compact storage shelving?

The columns stand eight and a half feet high instead of the standard seven and a half. The range aisles are roughly about twenty-two inches. Keyes Metcalf seemed to be concerned when I discussed this with him. He thought the aisle might be too narrow. It doesn't seem to be but it is not full, of course, and present use is very limited. After much experimentation, the building emerged as a structure adequate to take a second level of these stack ranges which should almost double its capacity. We have an open stack. Anyone who wishes may go there and browse. It is kept at a temperature that would be a little uncomfortable for working in the stacks, but there is an adjoining reading room. I asked the architect and engineers to come up with the economically optimum level of year-round temperature while maintaining roughly 50 percent humidity. They came out with something like fifty-five to sixty degrees; in fact it has been running just a little bit higher than we originally thought. Of course, it was never intended that anyone should work there except the shelver. We have had no trouble finding workers. As a matter of fact, the shelvers seem rather to like working there.

Since it is an open stack storage library, do readers have to go to the storage library for their books or may they request delivery to the central library?

The storage library is open from nine to five on weekdays and there is twice-a-day delivery to all existing service points on the campus, not only to Firestone but to any of the branches. The location of the book in the storage library—and this is really the important consideration to me—is indicated on all the card catalogs directly. Some institutions have tried to operate the storage library concept simply by charging out the collections at the circulation desk, but this method has seemed untenable to me. If the plan is to work effectively, the reader has a right to know why a book is not on the shelf where it belongs without going through the whole business of inquiring at the circulation desk. We are also maintaining the original shelf list in order by simply indicating on our shelf list the new and the old location so that a reader can see the collection in the shelf list as it ideally exists in classified order—just as if no books had been removed for storage or were loaned to others. We have never been able to sell the faculty and students on the idea of browsing through the shelf list, but I still hope to do this. Of course, all this recording may not be worth the cost at some future point.

One other thing may be worth mentioning to complete the physical description of our storage unit. We were dubious about it at first but now think it will work out very well. We shelve books by size according to five categories. The depth of the shelves also varies. Within the five sizes, the books are arranged in classified order, not in an arbitrary order. So it is possible to do a crude sort of browsing, if one wishes to, right at the shelves.

In our whole library concept the idea of browsing is important to our faculty and students. Of course, in the storage situation it is not very satisfactory because the user has five or six places to look. But it seemed to me that we could manage this with very little loss of economy. We must have a shelver to run the building when it is open. Until it is full, he is going to have time on his hands. There is no reason he shouldn't use this time to rearrange books on the shelves as needed. It will involve a constant process of minor shifting which will not add to our cost since the man has to be there in any case.

There are questions I should like to ask you about the impact of the recent student movement on the library. First, how can the library provide a greater voice for students in the affairs of the library?

It is a difficult area in which to generalize; so let me speak of our own situation. I have thought for years that we needed a student library committee. I wanted this committee, however, to be responsive to and representative of whatever form of student government we had. Now for local reasons on the campus, student government in the past has been very weak. It wasn't really very representative; it wasn't really very effective. Two or three years ago, originating with the students, there was considerable reform. We now have an Undergraduate Assembly which is highly representative. The composition of this group is made up on a rather carefully conceived basis. For example, different residential units have representatives. It isn't just an open election; it is a structured election; so it is quite representative of the different undergraduate elements on the campus. When we began to get that kind of student government, I turned to them and asked for the appointment of a small student library committee to advise me. It never worked very well, perhaps because I did not call on it enough, and perhaps because the climate of the campus was not very receptive to active student participation. With the new participatory democracy everywhere, this whole issue has taken on a completely new tone. For more than a year now, considerably more than a year, we have had at Princeton a faculty-student committee on the structure of the University. This committee has gone into all aspects of participation and the problem of how to reflect adequately the views of the University community. One of the early recommendations to come out of this committee was that certain faculty committees should be accompanied by parallel student committees, separate committees but parallel in structure with liaison between them, meeting together as seemed to be indicated, and at least keeping in touch with each other. I immediately expressed the hope that the faculty library committee would be equipped with one of these student parallel committees and this was done. A committee was appointed by the Undergraduate Assembly. We have had it for one year. After its first meeting with the faculty committee at the beginning of the year, the faculty committee immediately voted to invite the student committee to meet with it always, essentially as observers. The student committee participates fully in discussion, but it does not have a vote. But it can meet separately and cast its own vote. To my knowledge during the year it has never done this. The monthly meetings with the faculty committee have been very productive of ideas. They have given the faculty committee a better concept of what the students like and don't like about the library than it has ever had before. In my view this has been a very successful operation. I think perhaps a parallel committee with the full interchange between the two committees might be better than a token student representation on a faculty committee where it would be clearly out-numbered. There is no sense of tokenism in our situation. The students have their own committee with authority to speak to the University Librarian, the President, or to anybody they want. We have chosen to invite this committee to meet always with the faculty committee and it has worked very well.

What recommendations have the students made?

The first one had to do with lengthening library hours. The library was already open quite long hours, from eight in the morning until midnight, six days a week, and on Sunday from 2 p.m. until midnight. They found two periods when students wanted to get into the central library at hours other than these. Sunday morning they thought was a useful time; so we accepted their suggestion to open the library at ten o'clock Sunday morning. It has worked well and we shall continue to do it. The other need was not necessarily a library responsibility, but it concerned a reading room of some sort in the library open all night. We agreed to do this on an experimental basis in one room which had a separate outside entrance and exit door. Our reserve reading room, which is presently a conventional closed-stack reserve operation, had an outside door and was planned for after-hours use from the beginning. We could keep it open for late use without opening the rest of the library building. So we decided to try an experiment of leaving this room open past midnight until eight in the morning, with a careful check on occupancy each hour. It turned out that there was very little use after three o'clock in the morning, but quite justifiable use until three. So we went back to the committee, discussed the matter, and decided that except for exam periods, where we keep it open somewhat longer, we would close this room at three o'clock.

Have there been demands for access to the book collection as well as study quarters during the late hours?

Yes, for two reasons. First, we have a very large proportion of assigned individual carrels. We assign carrels to undergraduate seniors who in our particular set-up write a senior thesis and have occasion to collect library materials for use in the library. We have approximately one thousand assigned closed carrel seats in this library. Students were quick to point out that the study hall function does nothing for the man who is assigned to a carrel. Second, there are those who say they need to have access to the stack collection. So at the last meeting of this academic year, the students suggested that the faculty committee endorse the idea of trying an experiment to keep the central library open somewhat longer hours and to measure use. I am recommending this for next year to the University authorities who must decide on budgets and so forth. I do not know how it will come out, but so far we have been able to respond to all proposals of substance made by the student committee. Its function, of course, has been much more than that; there are many little matters which they do bring to our attention in free and open discussion.

If there are affirmative answers to all these requests, plus salary and book price rises, will not the quality of library service suffer in the long run?

It is quite possible. One simply has to balance and weigh the validity of the need. I have satisfied myself that the case just discussed is not just a whim. Students do use the library at these extended hours, and one could perhaps reduce it to a cost per student hour of library use, if one were mathematically minded, and ask what's it worth to have a student working in the library at an hour when he might not have worked otherwise. My own view so far is that we are within a tolerable limit on this. As I see it, our function is not just to build collections; our function is to get university students to use books.

When you speak of weighing the pros and cons you are suggesting the application of reason to these problems. From what I have observed of the present student climate, library hours, like segregation, are not a matter which can be dis-

cussed rationally. Libraries are going to have to extend their hours whether there is a rational justification or not. Am I right?

I would like to respond to that in this way. I would like to think there is a certain logic in acceding to the demands of students; in other words, that we shall not simply give in to everything they want because they want it. I think that much of what the students on this campus wanted during the past year, much but not all, has been good. They have perceived needs, legitimate needs in the curriculum, in the way we run the University, that I rather wish we had seen first. We have gained some perspective from our very active dialogue, to use that over-used word, with students this past year and a half on the campus. Now we have not done everything they wanted. There are some things they want which it is obvious we cannot do and some which we shouldn't.

May I put my question to you a little more specifically? The demand by black students for Afro-American studies has frequently been accompanied by a demand in some quarters for separate reading-room facilities in the library. How should a librarian respond to this kind of fragmentation, which I think you said you yielded to reluctantly in setting up a separate storage library?

Again, I think that I would say that this is a matter of balance in a particular situation. I think that I would like to avoid ideology here. In this situation let me say that at the moment we do not contemplate anything separate for our new Afro-American program. We have one under way, just started, under the supervision of a faculty committee. It will not be a segregated program in any sense; it will not be limited to black students. We have recruited, we think, a very able black professor to be the senior man in this program. It seems to us a legitimate area of academic study. Now, we have had a whole series of interdisciplinary programs at the University for a good many years. I think perhaps the earliest one was our American civilization program, which by now has become almost the traditional interdisciplinary program. Whenever possible we have tried to find a small separate room where a core collection of reference books and special reserves can be kept for each of these programs. It helps give the programs a sense of visibility, a sense of use; these small collections have been essentially duplicated and have not in that sense cut into the continuity of normal classification. We have what we call a graduate study room for every academic discipline which has its major collections in this building. The graduate study room is a small room which has the double function of a common room and a kind of beginning bibliographic center. Students spend a lot of their time there, see each other, and use special course reserves which are restricted to graduate student use. If the need came for something like this in the new Afro-American program, I would be quite sympathetic. It is in our pattern. We have some twelve or sixteen of these rooms now.

In this particular instance, I should think one of the difficulties would be to identify the material which would be placed in such an area.

I agree. I am not quite sure what one would put in such a room at the moment. We are not at all clear yet here as to what the literature of Afro-American studies is or ought to be. We have been trying for two years to build up our collection on the American Negro. We have made a special effort, secured a small foundation grant, and engaged a half-time curator for two years to develop these collections. This was before there was any special student demand. It seemed to us that here was an area where we were perhaps weak. We now think that we have very good general collections in the stacks and in pamphlet and file collections of fugitive material. If there were enough interest and if we could find the money, I think it would be quite legitimate to have a special curator and a special room.

You have one of the most influential and successful Friends of the Library organizations in this country. Can you give us a clue to the elements which make for success in establishing and maintaining a successful "friends" organization?

I am not sure that one can generalize on this subject, but let me describe briefly the concept of our own organization. In the first place Princeton is in a small community; the situation could be quite different in Atlanta, for example, where perhaps a higher proportion of alumni and friends are geographically contiguous. Our organization is really an international group of about 1,200 members, maybe 1,500 now—it seems to keep growing. We do not see most of the members at all; ours is a correspondence relationship. Members pay minimum dues of ten dollars. We try to keep dues low in contrast to other views of this sort of organization. What we are interested in is building a community of people interested in this library whom we will undertake to keep informed about our needs and so forth. Out of dues we receive a very small amount for acquisitions, perhaps five or six thousand dollars a year. The principle is very simple. When there appears to be a surplus in the operating account into which dues go, we transfer some of the money to an acquisition fund. So you see, we really have a lot of machinery producing very little money directly. Indirectly the results have been incalculable because we don't know what they have been, but I believe on balance they are very much worthwhile. In other words, in the course of a year we receive in dollars and collections about a million dollars in gifts. This does not all come from members of this organization, but I have traced back enough instances of gifts to be pretty sure that the maintenance of this organization has helped. It has created a climate which lets people know, people who have books, people who have money, and people who are interested in libraries, that this is an active and scholarly library. We publish the *Princeton Library Chronicle*, now in its twenty-sixth year, whose subscription is included in the dues, and we occasionally publish a book which either we give or sell to the Friends. The pattern here is to make available unique or scarce items which may exist in our own collections—essentially this rather than bibliographic.

Do your dues cover all costs of editing and publishing a journal?

The clearly identifiable costs are covered. For example, we have a membership committee, composed of Friends, outside the library. When they have a membership campaign, they do a mailing which is charged to the Friends' account. On the other hand, there is no question that there are many expenditures of the library in staff time which are buried in general library expenditures.

I am sure you devote a great deal of your time to this group. Do you have any staff time specifically assigned to the Friends' group?

Yes. The traditional pattern has been that the treasurer and the secretary of this organization are members of the library staff. In addition, the University Librarian is a vice-chairman. We keep a close eye on it. It is a very friendly working group, but we do assign particular staff members responsibility for keeping the organization going. The managing editor of the *Chronicle* receives a token salary.

What about those famous dinners which you once characterized as a seasonal activity exposing librarians to the occupational hazard of cirrhosis of the liver?

We have only one meeting a year, the annual dinner meeting. It attracts about two hundred to two hundred and fifty people. Most of them come from within the New York to Philadelphia area. It is a small number in proportion to the total membership but it is usually a very successful and pleasant kind of event. The Council, a group of about thirty, meets twice a year, once at the time of the annual dinner and again in the fall when the University Librarian is host to the dinner. I suppose the Council is really the group of donors and potential donors whom we cherish most highly. Our chairman is an alumnus and book collector who happens to live in Princeton.

I have heard complaints sometimes that Friends groups direct their interest to the rare items and showpieces while the library's real needs in research are neglected. How does one direct a Friends group toward supplying the library's most pressing needs?

In my experience, I think it would be folly to think that you would get much bread and butter from a Friends group. This is essentially a kind of rare books, special collections type of operation. That's what draws people together.

I was interested in reading in Dean Brown's new book, The Liberal University,* *that he regards the university library as "the Cinderella in university administration." He goes on to suggest that a renaissance of support "must come in the first instance from the faculty as both teachers and scholars." Such support he says "will never reach the decibels in tone of that for new faculty appointments or new areas of instruc-*

*Brown, J. D., *The Liberal University*. New York: McGraw-Hill, 1969.

*tion." Well, to ask professors to limit their curricula or to cut
down on their appointments is to ask them to govern themselves
by a different philosophy from that which prevails today. So
where does this leave the librarian?*

In the whole spectrum of university funding at Princeton
the library is only just behind the faculty. It is not in a bad
position. I think the faculty ought to come first. I am talking
now about the money needed to make sure that you have the
right kind of faculty. In our situation here, the faculty is the
key thing. And I believe it ought to be in most places. The
faculty ought to make sure, as Dean Brown is saying, that the
library gets the next cut. This next cut may be lower—it shouldn't
be very much lower. I had some illustration of this with a pie-
cutting operation we had during the last five years. When we
received one of the Ford developmental grants for area studies,
we set up a coordinating committee on foreign and international
programs, which was to decide how the Ford grant and other
money received for this purpose should be apportioned and
used. The committee broke down into subcommittees by region—
Slavic, Latin American, and so on. As University Librarian I
served as a member of the central committee. By and large
throughout this business, when it came to a firm and hard choice,
members of the faculty put the library second. Since the faculty
were available already in several of the departments, the priorities in this case went to graduate fellowships, then the library,
even though this meant throwing aside plans for expansion, even
expansion of the faculty, and all kinds of other things such as
summer travel grants, etc. All of these came lower than the
library. So it is my impression and my experience that with
most faculty members the library comes next after the faculty
themselves.

*Another problem facing librarians is the need for the con-
tinued education of professional staff members. There was a
time when we graduated from library school, took a job, and
remained in it until we retired or took a better position. Nowa-
days the job of the librarian is becoming increasingly specialized
and it is necessary to go back to school, or at least to refresh and
up-date one's knowledge constantly. If you agree that this is
an urgent need, have you any suggestions for resolving it?*

I agree absolutely. I am not sure that I think one accomplishes this by "going back to library school," but we must do something along the line of continued professional development—a mid-career kind of development. There are a couple of things which seem good to me. First, the Metcalf seminars at Rutgers a few years ago seem to have done a splendid job. Most of the young men who participated in those seminars have developed just as one hoped they would. Second, the recently approved Council on Library Resources fellowships offer the possibility of a stimulus for somebody in mid-career to take a few months off to carry out a project, not because it is something that needs to be done, but because it will benefit and broaden his growth as a librarian. As you know, the first round of these grants was just announced a few months ago, so that it is too early to tell. But that kind of thing is good. I think we should do more in the library field that is the equivalent of post-doctoral work in, for example, the natural sciences. This may be post-M.A. work rather than doctoral, not necessarily working for a degree but some kind of association with a research and educational institution in the library field. It might be in the computer field for a year or part of a year. Administratively, this means that somehow we have got to find ways of securing leaves of absence for librarians much more frequently than is the practice today.

What provision or progress have you made in this matter at Princeton?

When the University Librarian sees that there is a good reason for a leave of absence for a staff member, he can recommend it to the Dean of the Faculty, who will generally approve leave with pay, but with no provision for the replacement of the staff member in the library. This, of course, is the great weakness. Our faculty system is such that each department is overstaffed by a formula which in effect gives every member of the faculty a leave about every six years. It is not automatic. Leave with pay is obtained only upon submission to the department of a research proposal or something of the sort. So leaves of absence fluctuate greatly at Princeton. Some people, it seems to me, are on leave every other year and others do not go very often. But it is a flexible system which allows the man who has the initiative and energy to do something about it. This is what I think we need in the library. If a man is teaching, it is very often a useful thing to bring in a visiting professor. Princeton's faculty system provides the money to do that. For the library to bring in a head of the Order Department, for example, is not very satisfactory because it takes time, even for a veteran, to learn the routines. I see problems also in administration in having temporary people occupying administrative posts even if the funds were available.

Your plan of leave sounds very good and certainly clarifies the situation for everyone on the staff, but it sounds somewhat restrictive both as to person and project. Will this serve the purpose of encouraging a sufficient number of staff members to accomplish the purpose of continually up-dating their professional knowledge?

In the rules and procedure of the professional library staff (*Rules and Procedures of the Professional Library Staff of Princeton*), which is in a sense the library's constitution and bylaws, there is a section on leave which reads in part as follows: "In order to increase professional competence and to contribute to the advancement of learning, individuals may, in special circumstances, be granted up to a year's leave at half pay or six month's leave at full pay. Proposals for leave should contain a full account of the project. . . ." Now, the procedure is clear enough. The weakness in the statement as I see it is the phrase "in special circumstances." In other words, these leaves are not routine and since there is no provision in the budget for replacements they cannot be regarded as the normal thing. They are special. I suppose for the past four or five years we have had a person on leave for at least a part of the year under this arrangement, but with a professional staff of seventy-five people, this is not quite as many as one would like to have. Perhaps we should have ten people away every year. It is not just the problem of money that bothers me. I think we could sell the idea of funding leaves since the faculty arrangement is so well-established. There is also the administrative problem of how you handle it if you have the money.

You have been closely associated with international library matters in general and UNESCO in particular. What has librarianship accomplished through UNESCO?

My term with the U.S. National Commission for UNESCO

ended seven or eight years ago, so I am not up-to-date. My impression is this. UNESCO has done some useful, visible things such as the Delhi Public Library, a model pilot library. It has been wonderfully successful as a public library. It is a very exciting place; its branches are lively, busy. It's good. The difficulty is that it hasn't been imitated. The pilot concept has not worked there, or as far as I can see, in any of the other pilot operations. It doesn't work because the money is not there.

And this brings me around to what I really want to say about UNESCO. This reflects my own view after looking at foreign aid for a good many years, in the library and in related fields. I believe just as strongly as I did ten years ago that it would be to the advantage of the United States to give whatever aid it can afford multilaterally rather than bilaterally. We do not win friends by giving money. The object of giving money is to bring up the undeveloped parts of the world because it is to our advantage to do so in the long run. The best way to accomplish this is through a multilateral organization. UNESCO could be built up to this capability more than it has been or is today if we made the decision to put a larger proportion of our foreign aid money there. The UNESCO library budget is relatively tiny. On the other hand, if one travels around the world, wherever one goes, one finds evidence of UNESCO's influence. In 1958 I was in Iraq and a UNESCO library specialist had preceded me there. He had conducted some little seminars in simple basic library operations, and whatever knowledge of Western library methods those people had came from what this man had taught them. I think this was all to the good. In other words, a library presence in an international organization seemed to me an important and central kind of thing even if the visible results were not staggering at the moment. There is another difficulty which worries everybody who has ever had anything to do with these big international organizations, and that is the tremendous difficulty of getting more than a hundred nations to agree on what to do. This is part of the problem. Yet it seems to me that the business of getting nations to agree is an exercise which leads toward peace and all the other things UNESCO is supposed to do. So I think it is worth it.

If one wants to get a new library built in the middle of Africa, it is obviously easier for the United States to give the money and build the building than it is to do this through

UNESCO. But I think the total benefits are larger by doing it multilaterally. That's my view of UNESCO at the moment.

One final question, if I may. Isn't Princeton one of the largest, if not the largest, Eastern university library where the open-stack principle fully prevails? Since university libraries have suffered severely from loss and mutilation of books in recent years, I know that librarians and others interested in libraries will look to what you have to say about this matter. I wonder, also, if your readers are badly handicapped by mis-shelved and out-of-order books?

The loss and mutilation of books is a matter of great concern both to librarians and to the users of libraries. I would not like to generalize about libraries which are differently situated, such as those in the heart of the urban area, but I believe that our losses are not related to the fact that the vast majority of our books are on open stacks. Let me be specific. We have in the Firestone Library, our central building, a little over a million volumes on completely open stacks which anyone may enter without special permission. A guard at the exit to the building who checks books and briefcases as people leave is the only barrier. A perpetual inventory, involving a check of books actually on the shelves with the shelflist and the circulation records, occupies the full time of two non-professional staff members except for a portion of their time spent in attempting to trace books reported missing. One complete inventory of the open stacks in Firestone requires about eighteen months. One inventory turns up several thousand volumes which are missing. Some of these missing volumes, of course, may be temporarily misshelved or simply lying on a nearby table where they have been left during the same day. We do not count a book as lost until it turns up as missing on two successive inventories. At that time a decision is made whether to replace it or whether to withdraw the catalog cards. Urgently needed volumes are replaced immediately, of course, as they are discovered missing without waiting for the completion of this process. At any rate, our records, which I believe to be quite accurate, indicate that we actually lose about a thousand volumes in each eighteen-month period. This seems to me a tolerable price to pay for the pedagogical value of open stacks, and it is my impression that this rate of loss compares very favorably with that in closed-stack libraries.

Multilation, such as the tearing out of pages rather than taking notes, which seems to be increasing, is for us a more serious problem. I doubt however that this is affected much by open stacks, for the same thing can happen even after a book has been legitimately charged out. Perhaps the best response is public opinion, and we have stimulated editorials in our student newspaper, etc. Most readers are as infuriated by this practice as the library staff.

The other part of your question is whether in an open-stack library readers are badly handicapped by misshelved and out-of-order books. My answer is that I don't think they need be if the library puts the same amount of money into stack maintenance that it would put into a paging system in a closed-stack library. We have a staff of eight shelvers under the direction of the superintendent of shelves. Each is responsible for a specific section of the open-stack collections in Firestone and manages to keep the books in excellent order. The periodic inventory which I have just described also helps, of course. About once a year some member of the faculty mentions to me that the books in which he is particularly interested seem to be becoming disorganized. Upon investigation it nearly always turns out that the shelver responsible for that section has been ill or is incompetent, and remedial steps are taken.

I am saying simply that open stacks are not necessarily disorderly stacks, but that one must make an effort to keep them in order.

Robert B. Downs

ROBERT DOWNS is one of the comparatively few librarians of today of whom it can be confidently said that sooner or later there will be a *festschrift* volume published in his honor. Librarians are in his debt in many ways: he pioneered resources studies; he helped to establish one of the few notable efforts in library co-operation which has persisted since its establishment and contributed broadly to library cooperation; he has been a leader in university library administration and library education; he has been a notable representative of American librarianship abroad; and his many published works and philosophy generally express what every librarian hopes to express: the priceless contribution of the book and the contribution which the library makes to the usefulness and influence of books. His high sense of professional duty, his fairness as an administrator, and his unremitting effort in behalf of librarians and librarianship have won him a wide circle of friends not only in the library but in the academic world at large. His honorary degrees from Colby, Toledo, and Ohio State attest to his distinction at home while consultantships in behalf of the governments of Turkey, Brazil, Japan, Afghanistan, and Mexico bear witness to his reputation broad.

Educated at the University of North Carolina and Columbia University, he served as head librarian of Colby College, the University of North Carolina, and New York University before becoming Dean (formerly director) of the Graduate School of Library Science and administrative head of the University of Illinois Libraries in 1943. He was interviewed in Washington, D. C., on January 26, 1969.

You have been a champion of faculty status for librarians for many years. Have librarians made significant progress in securing faculty status in the fullest sense since you have been reporting these developments?

I think we are making rather steady progress in the direction of genuine faculty or academic status in the university library field, particularly in the state-supported institutions. Much less progress is being made in the private universities which have, generally speaking, approached this problem much more conservatively. One of the real breakthroughs, for example, has occurred at the City University of New York, which has gone all the way in giving its librarians faculty status, including the full faculty salary scale, with the result that CUNY has the highest beginning salary of any university library in the country. The State University of New York is now moving in the same direction. Here are two large groups of professional librarians in two systems who recently have been accorded full faculty status and all the perquisites which go with it.

These are two notable examples of what I think is happening all over the country. I am inclined to think that if a university does not give this kind of recognition to its librarians in the future, it is going to have increasing difficulties in recruiting the best people.

You say that private institutions are much more restrictive about extending faculty privileges to librarians. Why is this?

I think this is partly and perhaps mainly due to the influence of professors who resist bringing into the faculty anyone who is not a classroom teacher. The state university is more liberal in this respect. There is less homogeneity of background because of the wide spectra of curricula; hence less emphasis on the old idea of faculty being a "community of scholars."

Is it also true that state universities have more people engaged in research and other activities where teaching in the classroom is not a primary concern or may not be practiced at all?

Yes, this is true. State universities have agriculture extension agents, research faculty, editors, legal council, and people of this kind who do not hold classes. Many of these have faculty status.

Academic status among faculty has traditionally implied certain rights and privileges. One of the most significant of these is the right to effective involvement in the intellectual life and educational policy of the university. Has faculty status for librarians opened the way for this kind of involvement?

I can cite our own experience at the University of Illinois. A number of our librarians have become involved in educational matters and policy through serving on various committees of the several colleges of the University. In a way we are a group apart, but we are closely allied with the library school. Several of the librarians participate in the library school teaching program. It is probably true that we have more in common with the faculty of the library school than we do with other faculties on the campus.

Is it possible that you overestimate the involvement of the teaching faculty in university policy? More and more, it seems to me, faculty are becoming increasingly involved in research missions of their own, foreign assignments, writing, and consulting, so that they do not have very much time for educational policy. They are willing to leave this kind of responsibility to deans, directors, and other administrators. An example of this willingness to divest themselves of educational responsibility in library matters may be seen in current book selection policies. At one time the faculty thought that they should be responsible for all book selection. Now there are many who resent being bothered about this; they cannot see that time and energy devoted to book selection is going to help them advance their career in any way. The time and effort they give to the library is not credited to them by their departments. Rather, it is time taken away from their writing and research and so they prefer to leave this chore, as many of them consider it, to the professional library staff. There are probably no more than ten or a dozen faculty members at the University of Illinois who devote an appreciable amount of time to building library collections.

A characteristic of faculty which goes with their status is their concern for personal matters, the selection of new colleagues, salary, tenure, etc. Has this same right been transferred to librarians where they have been accorded faculty status?

I would question your assumption that the selection of a new professor in a particular department is a responsibility of his faculty colleagues. In many cases, I am certain, the selection and appointments are made by department heads who may consult with members of the faculty but who retain final responsibility for recommending appointment. At the University of Illinois we consult with department heads as well as with other librarians who are going to be working with the new appointees after they are appointed. Whenever a new librarian is being considered, the department head makes his recommendation, the associate director passes on it, and the personnel director reviews the applicant's credentials before it comes to me for approval. So I would say that in our own library situation, at least, four or five people are consulted when a new appointment is being made.

What you have described is essentially a hierarchical method of channeling recommendations up the line. What I am talking about has more to do with faculty resolving these problems among themselves. Take tenure, for example; I believe that in matters of tenure the faculty of a department will in the last analysis decide through their recommendations whether or not their new colleague is given tenure. A dean is not likely to approve or disapprove tenure contrary to the faculty recommendation of a department. Do you see librarians moving in this direction as they acquire faculty status?

It could very well be true. In the case of tenure, which you singled out, however, the director of libraries usually does not decide these matters by himself. At the University of Illinois a good many people are consulted on matters of tenure. As a matter of fact, after a certain period of employment, tenure at the University of Illinois is automatic for everyone, not just for professors and associate professors. An individual who has been in the service of the University for six years is either given tenure or is dropped.

You have made many library surveys and are an authority in this field. In a recent book on university library matters in Australia, the author observes that "there is no general agreement amongst librarians on the value of the library surveys." How do you feel about this?

Well, if I didn't think they had value, I certainly would not have become involved in as many as I have. You are probably acquainted with the E. W. Erickson study.* He examined the principal surveys which had been made from the 1930's on down to the early 1950's, visiting the libraries to see how many of the recommendations had been carried out. In an amazing number of cases, the universities had followed the recommendations of the surveyors.

From my own experience, I have found that many of the recommendations which we have made have been implemented almost immediately and, where there have been delays, the explanation has usually been a shortage of funds.

College and university libraries have participated widely in institutional self-surveys. Do you think that these surveys have helped to improve and strengthen libraries?

I have not worked with any of the self-survey groups, but I think they would undoubtedly have value. We are about to have our ten-year visit from the North Central Association, and for this purpose we are making some compilation of material from all divisions of the University. However, I do not think that this kind of approach to library surveying has any great depth. I think that one will get a much more objective survey by someone from the outside if he is really qualified to look over the library operation. It is perhaps another illustration of the prophet being without honor in his own country. If you have a surveyor of known reputation from outside come in to look at the library, the president and other administrators are much more likely to pay attention to him than they are to the local librarian, even though their recommendations are similar. In most cases, I think the local librarian really knows what the library's problems are and perhaps understands them

---

*E. W. Erickson, *College and University Library Surveys 1938-52*. Chicago: A.L.A., 1961.

as well as any outside surveyor, but he will not be listened to in the same way.

In the self-survey of the accrediting associations there is a follow-up by a visiting team which usually includes a librarian. This gives the survey some of the authority or status of an independent outside survey, does it not?

Yes, it does, but one of the difficulties in this approach is that the time of the visiting team is short and sometimes the library representative is well qualified as a surveyor and sometimes not.

Do you think the institutional self-survey with follow-up visiting teams is worth continuing as a regular part of the ac-creditation process? I'm thinking of the library aspect of the survey, of course.

It is a team effort and therefore the librarian who takes part in the visitation learns a good deal himself about the institution as a whole, makes new acquaintances among administrators and faculty of other institutions, and picks up ideas and suggestions. In my own case, I always learn a great deal from surveys. They are probably as useful to me in my own job as they are to the institution which I am visiting. I would certainly recommend in the regional accrediting program that the librarians of the visiting teams be selected with great care. They should have experience in surveying and they should know what to look for.

In recent years librarians have been very active in surveys, consulting, and in other types of missions which take them away from their campuses. What is the ethics of consultantship? What is so-called right action with respect to taking time from your job and being paid by another party?

The librarian has to weigh the situation and decide how much time he can legitimately give to this kind of extracurricular activity. It means that the librarian has to put in many hours making visits and writing reports, but I think it is defensible on two or three grounds. In the first place, if you are an experienced library surveyor you have some obligation to your profession over and beyond your primary job. If you can contribute to the advancement of library administration in this way, you are helping not only the institution you are surveying but librarianship in general. And then as I mentioned before, you learn a great deal during a survey which you can apply at home. I believe that I am a better library administrator from having participated in a number of such studies. Each library does something a little differently. From your observation of outside practices you may discover ways to correct deficiencies in your own situation. Of course, you have to keep in mind at all times that you cannot neglect your own work.

There is another point worth mentioning. Consulting has become a kind of national vogue, not only in libraries but in other fields. I have friends in engineering, chemistry, physics, and in various other fields who spend a great deal of their time away from the campus working for the federal government, state governments, industry, and business. They receive very handsome honorariums for these extra services. The University has a policy which governs such assignments and I think most faculty members follow the guidelines. On the other hand, I am quite certain that in a few cases the consultant neglects his local responsibilities and takes on more outside work than he should. In the case of the librarians, this probably does not happen very often and it should be said that we make the profession more attractive to able people if we encourage some outside survey work.

You have had unusual opportunities to serve and observe librarianship in foreign countries. I am sure that you have found this experience stimulating and useful in your career as a librarian. Do you think it would be helpful if comparative librarianship were required as a course in library school teaching today?

Offhand I would say that very few library schools pay any attention to comparative librarianship. Our American library schools concentrate on American practices. We perhaps egotistically consider that American libraries are the best in the world and that we do not need to pay any attention to what goes on anywhere else. And I think by and large that the rest of the world accepts us at our own valuation in this respect. Students abroad come to the United States to study librarianship if they can manage it. As I have visited abroad, it seemed to me that librarianship is at a rather primitive level in many countries. Their librarians can learn a great deal from American librarianship. I am not sure that we can learn much from them. I have argued this point of view with Dean Asheim who feels that we should accept them as they are and not try to judge them by our scale. It may be that what they are doing and the way they are doing it fits their needs. I do not accept this point of view except in a very limited degree. The librarians are very poorly paid and have no status; their book collections are frequently fragmented into small departmental or faculty collections; there is no union catalog and no one knows what the other library has—just all kinds of practices which I regard as pernicious. If they continue to follow these practices, they will never have good libraries.

Surely in European libraries, Canadian and Australian libraries, and in the libraries of some of the other countries there must be aspects of librarianship about which American librarians should be well informed. Do you not think the American librarian-in-training should have the broadening influence of a course which would acquaint him with some of the ideas of librarians elsewhere?

I would agree with this. My previous comments perhaps more aptly apply to the libraries I have observed in the Middle East and the Orient. The Canadian standards are quite comparable to our own. In some respects the British are ahead of us, for example in the field of library cooperation. Next year we are introducing a course in comparative librarianship at Illinois. There are other ways to cross international boundaries such as attending conferences and congresses, exchange of students in library schools, and informal visits to libraries abroad. A few years ago, as part of our seventy-fifth anniversary, we had an international conference on library education. The published proceedings show the state of library education in different countries and reflect in most instances the state of library practice in these countries. I might also mention that Dr. Lester Asheim gave a series of lectures on librarianship around the world, in our Windsor Lecture Program, which covers this same theme. These lectures were published by the University of Illinois Press under the title *Librarianship in Developing Countries*.

What are the important problems of recruitment for librarianship these days?

As you know, librarianship is still predominantly a feminine profession, about 85 percent women, even though there have been great changes in the past decade or so. This fact is reflected in salaries. If the proportion of men were higher, salaries would be higher. Recruitment is definitely affected by salary standards. In the college and university field, there is also the question of status. Recruiting would be greatly aided if we could change the popular image of librarianship as being for the lame, the halt, and the blind, for misfits, for people who have failed in other occupations. We need to spread the word of the range, diversity, and excitement of modern librarianship and the vast opportunities ahead.

Would you say that there is still a shortage of people entering the library field?

We are now getting as many students as we can handle in our library schools. This was not true four or five years ago. At Illinois, and I think in a number of other large schools, we are having to turn away a good many well-qualified people. We are trying to hold our enrollment down to about two hundred on a full-time basis. If we could accept more, we would have no difficulty in recruiting three or four hundred. So I do not think that recruitment is a major problem with us now. I doubt whether the so-called shortage of librarians is as acute now as it was five or ten years ago. This same question was raised in a discussion at a meeting of the Illinois State Board of Higher Education. Recently I said to Al Trezza, the Associate Director of the ALA, that library positions were being filled more easily than they were a few years ago. He looks at it from the point of view of the ALA and he says the shortage is almost as acute now as it ever was. From their point of view, and what they see and hear, the demand still far exceeds the supply.

Has the recent swing to technology in librarianship affected recruitment for librarianship? Faculty and presidents have been pressuring librarians to become more technologically minded.

The pressure that you speak of is certainly widespread. Faculty and university administrators think that librarians are quite backward in adopting the new technologies. They read all the science fiction about information storage and retrieval and then think that the librarian should develop push button systems which will give their readers instant access to all the information they require. As you know, the equipment for doing this simply does not exist at this stage and probably will not be available for a good many years to come except in certain kinds of library housekeeping operations. However, in the light of the publicity which has been given to this kind of thing, it is quite possible that young men who are inclined in the direction of science and technology have been attracted to the library field.

Another area of librarianship in which you have made a real contribution is in the field of publication. Recently in one of your Library Trend *issues, I read where a psychology professor stated that psychologists are interested only in what is just off the press, what is in the press, and what is now being written. He left the impression that so far as current psychological research is concerned, the library has only an archival function. Do you think this is true, and if it is, how are libraries to respond to the psychologist's need for current research materials?*

Well, the archival function is an important one. It cannot be ignored. The situation the professor describes is undoubtedly true in some of the sciences. For example, the head of our chemistry department recently mentioned that a man who had been out of the field for a year would have great difficulty in catching up. Things are moving so rapidly. That is why they have to stay on top of the literature all the time to see what the latest developments are. That is why the journal is so much more important than the book to the scientist.

But I gather that the psychologist I was quoting is really saying that the journal is not really important anymore for current psychological research.

I do not think this is true. It may be in his particular branch of psychology, but every science and every discipline must build on what has gone before. There is nothing completely new under the sun. The scholar in any field must have a sense of history, like Isaac Newton, who "by standing on the shoulders of giants" was able to see further. The past is best consulted through the printed word.

I notice that Science Citation Index *may refer to a particular scientist or professor rather than to an article. Presumably, if*

*you want the latest on a particular subject, you get in touch
with him directly.*

Well, I am sure that scientists consult each other a great
deal. You may remember that several years ago the A. N.
Marquis Company published a book entitled *Who Knows and
What*, locating the specialists in various subjects with the idea
of helping the user to get in touch with the specialist if he
needed the very last word on the subject. Marquis never got
out more than one edition of this work; so apparently it was
not a great success or at least there was not sufficient demand
to warrant a second edition. But there is no question that scientists
want the very latest information, and speed in getting that information to them is becoming increasingly an important characteristic of library service.

*To keep pace with this demand for currency requires a con-
stant increase in library acquisitions and in budgets. Is there any
established rate of annual financial support which a good university must maintain?*

Yes, I think there is, but first I would like to make the
point that the library is not growing any faster than other
divisions of the university. Actually the library percentage may
be going down rather than up. On the basis of increased book
and journal costs of the past few years, a university library is
going to need an increase in book funds of 15 to 20 percent
to keep abreast of faculty and student expectations. This would
cover inflation and the increased rate of publication. For the
past ten years book and periodical prices have been increasing
on an average of about 5 percent a year. And about twice as
many books are being published today as there were ten years
ago. This is a world-wide trend and not just limited to the
United States. According to UNESCO figures, the publication
rate throughout the world is going up. American research libraries
are becoming more and more involved in foreign acquisitions.
So taking all these factors into consideration, the university library book budget should be advancing at the rate of 15 percent
a year.

Are university libraries maintaining this rate of growth?

I think not, but there is no question that they are growing
much more rapidly than in the past. They have more money for

books and are adding many more volumes each year than in the past.

That raises a question in my mind. Some years back, immediately after World War II, we were saying that no one library could collect everything. We said that university libraries must be selective and must specialize. Today more than half the major libraries have blanket orders for American and foreign books. It looks as though we are really saying now that each library will collect everything of importance it can. Would you care to discuss this?

This is certainly a problem which all of us are very conscious of now. I think you are correct in thinking that we are getting away from the idea of selection and moving more in the direction of collection. We are certainly collecting comprehensively in the fields of primary interest, although we do not try to cover all subject fields. I have been very much interested in specialization for thirty years or more. At one time I was more hopeful that university and research libraries would move in this direction than I am today. It is a beautiful principle in theory: each library would develop specialities and develop these in strength while their neighbors and colleagues would develop other specialities. Well, this happens in actual practice to a very limited extent because the universities themselves refuse to specialize. Every university insists on covering the whole range of knowledge. The library is a service agency and if the faculty decides to offer advanced work in Sanskrit, or whatever the subject may be, the library has to support it. I recently made a study of a university library serving an institution which was rapidly extending its curriculum from a technological base to one which offered advanced degrees in all major fields, including the humanities and social sciences. The faculty brought in to teach the new courses was complaining about the lack of library resources. I discussed this matter with the president, who felt that the university could build up these courses without having strong library resources. In his opinion, the faculty could borrow or use what they needed at neighboring university libraries which were strong in these fields. This is totally unrealistic, of course. If an institution is going to offer courses at any level, it must provide the library resources to support them. On the other hand, the cooperative program between

Chapel Hill and Duke has worked out fairly well. These two institutions are somewhat complementry to each other and they are also only ten miles apart.

Doesn't this really boil down to the fact that the professor is more interested in his career and in promoting his discipline than he is in library development?

Yes. As indicated earlier, the professor's time is increasingly occupied by other pursuits. He is willing and anxious to have librarians take over the task of library development. He expects, however, that the book, or journal, or document he needs will be available when he wants it. In my view, this is not an undesirable phenomenon. Librarians *should* have the responsibility for building collections, and their assuming this will make for a stronger profession.

Robert L. Gitler

LIBRARIANSHIP is ever challenging and librarians are human. That message emerges clearly from an interview with Robert L. Gitler, University Librarian, University of San Francisco. Gitler is a dedicated librarian who believes with Robert Hutchins that "education may not save us, but it is the only hope we have." He got his start in librarianship at the University of California where he received a B.A. in political science and history and a graduate certificate in librarianship from the dean of deans of library schools, Sydney B. Mitchell. Later he received an M.S. in library science from Columbia University.

Gitler came to his present position after serving in a variety of places and positions. He was assistant librarian of San Jose State College Library, director of the University of Washington School of Librarianship, founder and director of the Japan Library School at Keio University, Tokyo, executive secretary of the ALA Library Education Division, director of Library Education at the State University of New York at Geneseo, and director of the Peabody Library School at George Peabody College in Nashville.

Among his numerous honors and awards are an honorary Ph.D. from Keio University, the Fourth Order of Merit with Cordon of Rising Sun from the Japanese government, and the Beta Phi Mu Award for distinguished service in education for librarianship.

The interview was conducted in Mr. Gitler's office on July 6, 1968, in the Richard A. Gleeson Library of the University of San Francisco, where he sat surrounded by shopping bags full of plunder which he had just brought back from the ALA meeting in Kansas City. All of this material he will read and re-read and pass on to his staff. He has great warmth, optimism, cheerfulness, and a tremendous capacity for work.

One thing I am anxious to talk with you about is your work in establishing the first university-level library school in Japan. As background to that, would you speak briefly of your involvement in this pioneer school?

When invited by the ALA to assume responsibility for this assignment—locating the school, determining the initial American faculty—I had some reservations.

First, how effective might one be in Japan without knowing the people's language—having to teach, communicate, negotiate through interpreters? Second, since the ALA had contracted for the project through the offices of the Department of Orientation for Occupied Areas of the Department of Defense, I wondered about the degree of free action an American faculty might have, even though the American-Japanese Peace Treaty, terminating the Occupation, already was drawn and about to be effected. And third, did the Japanese librarians really want a troupe of visiting librarians at that stage? After all, the Occupation years had brought a not inconsiderable number of foreign specialists in all fields to that defeated and occupied, but recovering, land. Might we not bear the onus of being academic or bibliographic carpetbaggers?

There were two schools of thought, pro and con, whether we could be effective working through the interpreter medium. Both views or theories are correct—depending upon the expertise of the interpreter, the patience and thoroughness of the foreign teacher, and the rapport and dedication of both. If these elements are conspicuously present a faculty can succeed, as was demonstrated. But there must be very real effort and vigilance on the part of all concerned, for carelessness and relaxation can result in slipshodness, can vitiate the arduous process. Second, as to whether there really would be academic freedom, or that we might have to clear through certain government agencies, American and Japanese, our writings for publication, our course outlines, etc.—this proved to be an unwarranted concern. Never have I worked in a freer academic milieu and situation, with no evidence of restraints such as the American universities experienced during the post-World War II would-be "purges" by certain state legislatures of liberal-minded faculty at some institutions. Complete and absolute freedom of thought and performance prevailed.

As to the third question, the degree of welcome—or reservation—with which we might expect to be received by the Japanese, I would be less than honest were I to state that we were greeted with acclaim or enthusiasm. A few library leaders did indicate their real interest in having the projected library school established and carried forward. But rank-and-file Japanese librarians greeted us politely, to be sure, but with a certain coolness. And this became understandable when we learned the cause of their apprehension. Because of the then new 1951-1952 Library Law, which set forth certain specifications including personnel standards, many Japanese librarians believed that we had come to train librarians to meet these new standards, and that they themselves would be displaced by the graduates of such a school. It took some time to overcome this concern, but overcome it was; not by pious statements or rebutals, but rather simply by the entire staff ignoring this thinking—although being on the *que vive* regarding it—and demonstrating through their personal continuing dedicated interest in, and assistance to, the in-service corps of librarians the country over that such was not the case.

Well, I cannot really continue on this without it becoming a speech or an essay on the many facets relating to the Japan Library School. And this is hardly appropriate for this interview.

One of the important things you did at Keio was to arrange to work your American faculty colleagues out of a job, including yourself, by replacing them with your Japanese counterparts. How was this managed and were you successful in finding qualified library school teachers in Japan to take your place?

Although the initial plan was that the American director and faculty be in residence for not more than fifteen to eighteen months at the most, with a Japanese faculty taking over thereafter, it became clear to me within six months after the school's opening that a much longer time—a period of years—would be required to develop a Japanese faculty that would be able to secure itself within the university's framework and administration. After all, we have problems enough in these United States finding faculty adequate in numbers and excellence. How much more this was so in Japan, with a limited tradition and background in library education, you may appreciate.

To continue briefly: I proposed a long-term (five years) plan whereby there would be continuing recruitment in diminishing numbers annually of American faculty, while at the same time sending abroad for graduate study in library science promising Japanese with strong potentials for leadership, teaching, and research in librarianship. These candidates could be selected either from in-service Japanese library personnel from over the country or from the Library School's (Keio University) graduates. Among approximately a dozen such fine persons all but two were Japan Library School graduates. And all are presently participating in the School as faculty or staff. It was a sort of implementation of the "Ten little Indians, then there were none" jingle, in that we replaced one American faculty member with a Japanese faculty member each year, the director being the last in the process to go. This whole long-range plan, together with a subsequent one for three additional years, was made possible by grants from the Rockefeller Foundation and Keio's annually increased financial participation.

At the time you established the school at Keio not many Japanese had professional library training and few had any concept of librarianship as a profession. Even during the 1960's when I was there for a short time, the rank and file of librarians were still concerned that they had little more than a clerical status. Has the Japan Library School helped to bring about a recognition of the professional contribution of the librarian? Do many of Keio's graduates hold the head librarian position in college and university libraries, for example?

It is still true that Japanese librarians and librarianship have a long way to go to achieve recognition and status. But I believe this is coming, that it is improving. Particularly has the advent of automation and the computer helped to bring about a new awareness of the role of the librarian, the information specialist.

Business and industry have been quick to develop special libraries, computer related activities, and have turned to Keio for its Japan Library School graduates. Medical librarianship is another area where Keio graduates are leaders in the field. But Japan Library School graduates have not played a correspondingly strong role in the academic and public library fields, as tradition there still holds the librarians in a rather subordinate role. There are some notable exceptions, but they are exceptions. Yet Keio's early contribution to school library development is still recognized and its faculty's counsels are sought by the dynamic head of the Japan School Library Association, Mr. Yataro Matsuo.

You spoke on the phone yesterday of the strong support which you have received from your administration at the University of San Francisco. Unfortunately, this is not typical of university library-administration relationships. Will you be more specific about your own situation and offer a suggestion as to what librarians may do to strengthen their relationship with administrators?

I think there exists a unique aspect here in that the administration is aware that the library must progress to match the burgeoning situation of the institution as a whole. For many years the library was a very small, conservative operation; the amount of money spent on the collection was negligible in relation to its program. In the last three or four years, the University has become coeducational and the enrollment has increased four to fivefold. The whole role of the University has undergone change and consequently the library must expand and change also. So when I came here, the administration was ready to support a high level of library service. Also, they were aware of a personal situation in the library which they were anxious to resolve as soon as possible. Consequently, they had a special interest and concern in the library. For the last three or four years, the library committees has been given the charge to enrich the collection and discover its weaknesses.

Do you report to the president?

Yes, but through the academic vice-president. I have had two informal conferences with the president since I came, but on this campus every administrative officer and academic head of a department reports to the academic vice-president. For example, before I could get a new salary schedule approved, which was a special percentage over and above the percentage increase provided for the University as a whole, the academic vice-president had to clear it with the president. We have close relations; he will call me up from time to time. For example, if he has an important visitor on the campus he may call up and say: "Mr. _____ is on the campus. I would like to bring him over, Bob." His use of the first name gives one a very warm feeling.

So you think that good library relations with the university administration are largely a personal matter?

Yes, and in addition to that, there is great pride in this library, an awareness of the role of the library. To return to your original question about strengthening this relationship, I should like to backtrack a little. Some years ago, because my work in education for librarianship brought me to the coast, I came to know some of the administrative officials at the University of San Francisco who were concerned about their library education program. Also they would talk to me about library administration. About three years ago when I was in the city, I happened to be out on the campus visiting Sister Mary Alma regarding her library credential program and she mentioned that our academic vice-president, Father Paul J. Harney, had said if I happened to be in town he would like to talk with me. So I went over and found that they were discussing the place of the library in the university and the role of the librarian. Father Harney asked me what I thought the librarian's role was. As a library educator I told him my thoughts, and I finished by pointing out that the librarian must be a person who is part of the entire operation, one who is well informed regarding the curriculum and administrative development of the university. At that time the librarian had no faculty status and was not a part of the councils. I mentioned that the librarian should sit in the senate, that he should have some relation to the curriculum committee, and that when changes in programs were being developed he should be so informed. I also pointed out that he should have full professorial status, with commensurate salary, so that he was one of the whole administrative group. Later, when this position was being developed, the librarian became part of all of this. The librarian is now a member of the senate, a full professor, and sits on a number of University committees such as the computer committee, advisory committee to the academic vice-president, and several others. The professional librarians now have what we call academic status, take part in all the academic processions, and have representation in the senate with provision for persons elected by the library staff on the same basis as the faculty.

Do you think that a general statement on library governance covering the points you have mentioned and others would be helpful in making the library a more effective service agency on the campus?

Any statement that helps to clarify the role of the librarian in the university complex is good. In my experience elsewhere, I have been part of the faculty in situations where I have seen the librarian out in left field. There were meetings about programs, degrees, curricula, and so on, where the poor old librarian was not represented and consequently knew nothing about what went on. Accordingly, I think such a statement would be useful where the administrators have not been library-oriented. Certain of our policies have been codified. For example, our faculty handbook states that the university librarian shall be appointed by the president and have the authority for the administrative direction of the entire operation of the Gleeson Library and any branch libraries except the School of Law. It also provides that with the advice of the faculty library committee the librarian shall be responsible for the development of library policies and planning, both immediate and long range. It emphasizes that the librarian shall be kept abreast of all university programs and plans.

If students wish to participate or be involved in library administration, should their wish be recognized as a legitimate claim both from the point of view of involvement and educational experience. If so, how is this to be effected?

I think the question is very pertinent because this is a phenomenon which is occurring all over these United States. At present we have a student representative on the vice-president's advisory committee and two representatives from the student body in the academic senate. We have not as yet a student representative on the library committee, but I envisage that there may be a request for it and we would certainly go along with it. When we had a sit-in last semester I was able to evolve with the students a voluntary operation by means of which they took over the library at 10:30 p.m. on the main floor and developed a voluntary committee to supervise matters. They did a beautiful job. Several of the staff were worried about what was going to happen, but I had complete confidence in the students and tried to demonstrate this in my relations with them. The result was successful, and I received a fine letter from the student body president, unsolicited, about how effective it had been.

The students then extended the hours of library operation after 10:30?

They wanted it on a twenty-four hour basis but we compromised on midnight. They carried the extended hours on a voluntary basis without my budget being involved. All they asked for was the main floor and a quiet place to study.

Are you doing any teaching of library school courses at the University of San Francisco?

No. I have deliberately refrained from injecting myself into the library education program here because this University is not yet ready or able to support adequately a full-blown graduate master's degree program at this time. For almost a decade they have done a satisfactory job with their school library credential program, to be sure. Time permitting, I would enjoy teaching a course. But not only does the university librarianship still require all my attention, but my entering or participating in the credential program would most certainly be construed that the University of San Francisco is under way in its plan to open a graduate library school—which it is not, at least not now. Even though I have been nine months in my present position, it has been difficult to dispel the idea that I was brought to the University of San Francisco to set up a library school. But this summer the University sponsored an institute on contemporary Japan, with a number of visiting professors, and I was invited to do a unit. I called it "Books and Libraries, Japanese." I enjoyed it very much.

I know you are in touch with library school developments even though you have left this field for the time being. Do you think one can do justice to the traditional courses in library school, such as reference and book selection, and at the same time give proper attention to the emerging courses in the applications of technology to librarianship?

This is a very important question. Forgetting about automation for the minute, the whole concept of librarianship has so many ramifications that the one-year program is almost impossible to manage. I think we have to expand and develop beyond a one-year program. We threw out the old fifth-year post-baccalaureate program and a sixth-year master's, which many of us felt was a mistake. That, of course, is water under the bridge. But now we are going back to special six-year programs with certificates, and heaven knows what. The only alternative is to go into the undergraduate program in a limited way, perhaps for the basic reference and cataloging courses. You could give these in the junior and senior years without robbing the undergraduate curriculum too much, and this would give you some room at the upper level for extra courses. People who don't have the basic courses will just have to take them before they come into the program.

From your experience in your present position and your meetings with colleagues in the area, what would you say are the important problems confronting the University of San Francisco library?

The tremendous rising costs of everything—the fact that we need to buy heavily here in order to build the collection. We are even allowing 11 percent for inflation each year. If you add 11 percent, you can only buy just what you had and you are lucky to just keep going. Then another point is we are in a large metropolitan area. To what extent should we become part of a cooperative system. Along that line we have just become involved in the Bay Region Catholic Institute of Higher Education Librarians. We are working to develop a union list of serials in these institutions in the Bay region so that we will not buy the same things. Right up on the hill here is Lone Mountain.* We have been taking *Chemical Abstracts;* they have been taking *Chemical Abstracts.* Well, they quickly stopped it. We have opened our resources so they may use our library;

---

*San Francisco College for Women.

this is quite a drain on our resources. We have not yet had full reciprocity because their new building is not yet ready. I have given instructions to our serials people that we must not duplicate any current subscriptions or back runs of periodicals which are held by the library on Lone Mountain. Then, of course, the occasion arises when a publication requested is not there but is held by the public library. Should we depend on the public library, for example, for the back file of the New York *Times?* Should the faculty be asked to go down there? The public library closes at nine o'clock. These are some of the hurdles to cooperation.

Consortiums are perhaps the answer to some of these problems. This last year we became a part of the Hoover Institute consortium, which is trying to secure a federal grant and foundation support to provide funds for traveling and fellowships for scholars of the institutions whose libraries are part of the consortium. We would like them to be able to live there, to do their research there, and to use the materials there. If a grant is approved, this can be done without any cost to the institutions themselves.

The real problem in cooperation is how far to go in building up your resources in relation to the other libraries in the area.

I have known you for a good many years. It seems to me that you have always sought out jobs both in the library field and outside where there has been a challenge to contribute not only to your profession but to humanity as well. I shall not ask you to comment on your war record but have you sought positions which offered this extra challenge or is this a figment of my imagination?

It is a figment of your imagination, by and large! I confess to having found the challenges that were in evidence in certain situations attractive. What I seem never to have learned, however, is that they usually proved to be akin to the visible portions of the icebergs, the really deep problems being hidden below the surface.

I often have wondered whether my having been born on a Saturday—I shall let you research that adage—may not be the propelling mystique guiding me into such situations, rather than any keen insight or bravura on my part.

David Kaser

DAVID KASER received his B.A. from Houghton College (1949), M.A. from the University of Notre Dame (1950). and his A.M.L.S. and Ph.D. (English) in 1952 and 1956, respectively, from the University of Michigan. During World War II he served with tank battalions in Alaska and Europe. He practiced librarianship in his home state for a number of years before going to Washington University as chief of acquisitions, rising to assistant director of technical services, a position he relinquished in 1960 to become director of the Joint University Libraries at Nashville. In the summer of 1968 he left his post at Nashville to become director of the Cornell University Libraries. Hard-working, persuasive, and quite certain in his own mind of his objectives and methods, he uses extroversion and ebullience—two qualities not commonly found in librarians—as weapons in a rapidly rising career.

Dr. Kaser has contributed extensively to his profession both in committee work and writing. His books include *Messrs. Carey & Lea of Philadelphia* (1957); *Joseph Charless, Printer in the Western Country* (1963); compiler of *Directory of the St. Louis Book and Printing Trades to 1850* (1961); and editor of *The Cost Book of Carey & Lea* (1963); and *Books in America's Past* (1966). He has published many articles in library, historical, bibliographical, and literary journals. He has also served as editor of the Missouri Library Association *Quarterly*, assistant editor of *Library Resources and Technical Services*, and from 1963 to 1969 as editor of *College and Research Libraries*.

The following interview took place in Washington, D. C., on January 26, 1969.

How did you come to select library work as a career? Did you by any chance work in a library as a student in college?

Yes. I was going to school on the GI bill after World War II. I had two years of college before the war and started back as a junior. Needing some extra money, I went over to the library and applied for a job. I remember the librarian gave me a long hard look and said: "We never had a man work in this library before." But after she thought about it and after she elicited from me an implicit guarantee that I would keep my hands off the women, she decided to give me a trial, for four weeks as I recall it. So she took me back into the stacks and introduced me to a Miss Jewell, who was a student assistant also. She had already worked there for a year and a half, I believe, so she was assigned to teach me everything I needed to know about pasting pockets in the backs of books, shelving, and what not. I worked there for two years, and subsequently I married Miss Jewell. I worked as a student also when I was studying for my master's degree at Notre Dame, and at the University of Michigan before I decided to become a librarian.

What college gave you such a good start?

It was Houghton College in New York State. And then, as I mentioned, I worked as a student assistant at Notre Dame and also when I was working on my doctorate. All this, incidentally, was long before I contemplated becoming a librarian.

At what stage in your academic career did you decide to become a librarian?

As I remember it, I was just about to complete the residence requirement for my doctorate. My field was English, and increasingly I came to feel that I did not want to teach English, which was about the only thing I could think of that somebody with my academic background might do. As I became increasingly uneasy about the future, my wife pointed out that English was a good field to have in the background for librarianship and that since I had already worked five or six years as a student library assistant, and seemed to enjoy it, then perhaps I should consider the library field. This was the first time such a possibility had ever occurred to me. So before I finished my doctorate, I went to library school and got a master's degree in library science.

Did you make much use of the library as an undergraduate?

You may recall that there is a military college at Dahlonega, Georgia. It was fully military in my time and maybe still is. Well, it is said that they erected a bronze plaque to me there—the unknown cadet—for using the library, but not in the way you mean. The librarian was the most conservative of persons. The idea got around that any cadet who let go a rebel yell in the library would be some kind of campus hero. Everybody was trying to get up nerve to do this so one day I marched in, did it, and marched out and no one ever found out who it was. So yes, I guess you could say I used the library.

How about library instruction? Did you receive any instruction in the use of the library by the librarian?

Yes, I believe that I received fairly good library instruction for its day in high school. I used the public library extensively; even when I was a little boy I used to go down to the public library and look at stereopticon slides. You remember when the public library used to keep stereoptican slides? But then in college I had some library instruction, and also in graduate school an excellent course in bibliography and research methods in English before I ever contemplated becoming a librarian. But I must admit that when I came to work on my dissertation, I wondered how anyone could write a dissertation in a subject field without first having training in library science. I had a great advantage over my colleagues who had started out with me; they didn't know how to use the library and I did.

What motivated you to seek your doctorate after you had a master's degree in librarianship? You must have felt a strong urge when you completed the library degree to begin practicing what you had learned.

Well, remember first of all that I was halfway through my studies for the doctorate when I began the master's in library science; so I was already well along in the work for an advanced degree. However, I think the motivating force was simply that I had already concluded that my future was going to be in university librarianship as opposed to public or even college library work. Therein were the challenges of librarianship which I found exciting. And as I looked around at people who were working in universities at that time—whether librarians, presidents, or faculty members—the taking of an advanced degree seemed to be something that most of them had done. Also as I talked with young faculty members in the teaching departments—persons with whom I had grown up who were a couple of years ahead of me or coming along behind me—they always somehow seemed to indicate that they were more comfortable with librarians who had doctorate degrees. Faculty are self-conscious people, shy people. I often think that this is the reason they are faculty. They are afraid to leave the university. The university is a nice home. They feel protected; they feel secure and safe. This is a paternalistic attitude resulting from the monastic origins of the university. They grow up in it, go on and on in the school, and they stay because they do not have to go out to face the world. And when they come up against a librarian who has gone through this same apprenticeship, they assume that he understands more clearly their problems and needs than anyone else. Now, we know that that is not necessarily true, but they feel more comfortable about it. And I think that anything we can do to make the faculty feel more comfortable is time well spent.

Whom did you regard as outstanding when you first entered the library field? What quality made him or her great?

There was really only one major name at this time that stood out in my mind above all others. This was William Warner Bishop. I was at Ann Arbor at the time and even though William Warner Bishop had retired, eight years before if I recall correctly, nonetheless he was still around the building and his personality dominated the whole library scene there. And the qualities that struck me at the time about Dr. Bishop were his sound scholarship, his leadership in library matters at the University of Michigan from 1914 to 1942, and his initiative and counsel in making librarianship an international discipline. Twice he had been president of the International Federation of Library

Associations. These qualities of Dr. Bishop prompted me to keep looking back at him and to ask: "How did he do this"? If I had a goal at that time, I suppose it was to try to be like William Warner Bishop.

Would you say that today the quality of educational or scholarly competence, which you admired in Dr. Bishop, has declined while such things as personality and management skills have increased in the field of librarianship?

The question sounds at bit cynical but I am sure you do not mean it that way. Yes, I suppose there is some truth in your comment. But I certainly think management skills are more important today than they were in the past, perhaps personality also. We have long recognized that academic libraries have doubled in size every sixteen years or whatever the formula is. I think we are not always so ready to recognize the corollary to that which is that as libraries double in size they are double in complexity and difficulty of use and management. This fact, that libraries are doubling in complexity every sixteen years, is bound to require a higher level of management skills. The libraries today must present a much broader range of challenges and problems to solve than libraries did thirty-five years ago. This fact alone necessitates greater management skill.

You are saying then that there are techniques of management which one can learn; that good library management is not just a matter of integrity, patience, and common sense?

Well, I think good management must, to a substantial degree, have the characteristics you mention but I think there are also techniques which one can learn and apply. There are techniques of leadership which one can learn almost out of a book. I think the fact that the army has leadership schools to which to send prospective corporals for three days is evidence of this. I think we could do the same thing for library supervisors, and have done it, incidentally. I think we have all seen tragic situations where a good person without preparation is put in charge of something and then falls on his face. I think there are skills which one can develop. Sometimes these are on a very rudimentary level where one is supervising three student assistants and sometimes they are on a substantially more complex level. Yes, I believe there are techniques of management.

Back in the 1930's and 1940's we were severely criticized for being too much concerned with the techniques of our work and not enough with books and the content of books. We seem to be even more concerned today with techniques, with the business of developing a smooth and fast-running automation. Are we in danger of neglecting our major scholarly functions?

Maybe I misinterpreted the question here, but it seems to me that the person who goes into university librarianship—for the most part to abet scholarship whether as reference, circulation, or acquisitions librarian—is on the firing line working with faculty for the accomplishment of the ends of the university. The librarian is there so that the faculty member can do his business, whatever that is. The librarian aids the professor in his individual research and as such is a participant in his scholarship. If the librarian can speed up his service through a kind of mechanized activity, it does not seem to me that this makes his service any less valuable. On the contrary, it seems to me that it makes librarianship more valuable. The "mechanized" librarian aids scholarship better by securing and producing more books more rapidly than he could otherwise do.

My question stems from the feeling that the constant current emphasis in librarianship on mechanization and the continuing pressure for speed-up in service has varied and subtle effects upon a library and library staff. Building collections and assisting readers may still be the librarian's function, but the technological paraphernalia may become overwhelming.

I think what the librarian has to do in a case like this is to take a broader view of what it is he is doing. If he thinks that all he is doing is standing there pushing a button, then he is no more professional than the man who puts the hub caps on automobiles. If he is building a car or building a research project, this is something else. He is a participant in that project. If he takes the limited view of what he is doing, he is merely a technician. I cannot imagine a person, however, going through the library education program that is available today and coming out with such a limited view of what his responsibility is.

Well, let me put it another way. It is very difficult to pick up a library journal or attend a library institute today which is not largely devoted to the computer or some cousin of the computer and its application to librarianship. Now the tragedy of this to me is that most librarians who have come into the profession to find inspiration, wisdom, delight in books, and the conveyance of this pleasure and wisdom to others are now reduced to making change for Xerox machines, exit control systems, automating circulation, and the like. What sort of recruit is this kind of mechanical operation going to bring to the field?

Well, I am not sure that I agree. No sir, I don't. I think I know what you mean, however. You mean that you pick up a journal today and eight of the ten articles deal with the use of complex formulae for long-range planning, simulation and mathematical modeling of library problems, and so forth, and you say "where is the library in all this?" I understand that. But I think again that the overall purpose of the library involving itself in these things is to enable it to fulfill better its humanistic responsibility. The library is still primarily a humanistic laboratory and the way in which the information is transferred doesn't make it any less humanistic. The humanistic activity of the library persists regardless of whether the material is handed across the desk by hand or whether it is transmitted over some kind of cable.

Now as to the kind of people who are being attracted into librarianship, I think that we are getting new kinds of disciplines represented in the library field. This is healthy. We have needed them in the past. Some of the young people coming to us today would have seen no place in the library field for their interests and knowledge in the past. Quite often these are persons trained in disciplines which are new to society generally. We are getting communicators, planners, and computer people. We need these people.

A characteristic of university libraries in the late 1960's is the comprehensiveness of their collecting in practically all fields. Back in the 1930's and 1940's we acknowledged that no one could collect everything; we talked a great deal about selectivity versus comprehensiveness and introduced the idea of cooperative specialization. It looks to me as though today we are closing our eyes to the fact that we simply cannot go on collecting on this scale individually—either financially or in terms of space. What is your opinion?

It does appear that we think we can collect everything in all the major university libraries but even though we may be acting this way I do not think we really believe it. While we are collecting as rapidly and comprehensively as possible, we are also scrambling just as fast as we can to eliminate the necessity for doing so. Many of us are investing every penny we can lay our hands on to establish library networks and develop rapid communication devices. No one will deny the importance of the research library industry as a whole collecting comprehensively, but all will also concur that individual libraries can never afford to do so in all fields. Regrettably, there is some overlap in the collecting policies of quite a few major libraries, but much is also eliminated by cooperative agreement. At Cornell, for example, we are collecting everything that we can get out of Southeast Asia, but Yale is not and Harvard is not, and Stanford is not because they know Cornell is. At Cornell, on the other hand, we are not collecting Africana because we know that Northwestern is collecting Africana. Increasingly university administrators are coming to recognize the enormous library price tags on new academic programs and are refusing to initiate programs unless there is reasonable cause to believe the library will be able to support them. This, I think we all will agree, is healthy.

You are saying that if the faculty at Yale decided to promote an institute in Southeastern Asian studies, the library at Yale would not develop a major collection in this field?

I do not believe they would ever attain the strength of Cornell's unless we abdicated our responsibility to it. Every once in a while an institution establishes a new program and consequently the library has to increase its level of collecting. It may increase from a "D" level* to a "C" level or even to a "B" level, but to begin now to collect comprehensively, to collect on an "A" level, would hardly seem possible unless it is in a field where no one is yet collecting at the "A" level, and it is difficult to conceive such a field, although I expect that there are some.

---

*The designations "A", "B", etc., have no specific meaning but are cited to show the spread in building a university library, ranging from a basic information collection to a comprehensive research collection.

Assuming that universities are not going to duplicate area studies which demand duplication of "A" level collecting, do you think libraries are going to be able to house all the material they are now collecting?

Well, as you know, library growth is charted on an exponential curve, a curve upward. I think that just as the growth curve rises, there is another curve developing out there, which might perhaps be plotted, coming down on us. That second curve represents such factors as rapid copy transmission and machine bibliographic control. We do not know just when these devices will be here to help us, but hopefully they will come to our rescue before we outstrip our building ability entirely. So I believe that the thrust of rapid growth which we are going through now will eventually decelerate as a result of automation, hopefully within a decade.

If we turn for the moment from the larger university library to the smaller university library or even to the large college library, I am reminded of a recent article by Arnold Sable in which he said book selection is dead. He goes on to explain that large book funds, government grants, blanket orders and the like have eliminated the need for selection. In the past book selection has been generally considered one of the intellectual crutches of the library profession. What happens when that is pulled out from under us? It takes the fun out of librarianship, doesn't it?

I'm going to beg off on that one if I may because I have not had experience in college libraries, so I do not really know the answer. I can say, however, that from a theoretical standpoint at any rate I cannot conceive how a college library book collection can be good except as it has been rigorously selected against a very carefully designed list of canons, and weeded constantly to reflect fluxing curricular needs of the institution.

Universities are having to take into account student power these days by appointment of students on committees, seeking their advice on this and that, and so on. How does the library make its adjustment to the recent student demand for involvement?

Students have always needed something to demonstrate about, and I suppose if we conceded something to them before they asked for it they would simply have to find something else to ask for. Universities have been very paternalistic in their attitudes toward students, and I am doubtful if students need this kind of paternalism. If we have not involved students at Cornell more than we have, it is only by default of the students. They have not asked to be involved. We would be perfectly happy to involve them much more fully.

Well, regardless of the type of involvement, it appears to me that student involvement in the library sooner or later boils down to a demand for longer library hours. How do you feel about this?

I think that this is justified. If we are not staying open twenty-four hours a day now, it should be only because no one has asked us to. It is clear that there are students who study around the clock. At any hour day or night there are a fair number of students around a campus somewhere studying. It seems to me that in the past we have scheduled libraries to meet the needs only of day people like myself. I'm not good for anything much after nine o'clock at night. So the library begins to run down at that time and eventually at eleven or twelve we cut off the lights and throw everybody out. But there are also night people. There are people who only get going good about the time we lock the doors. We are doing them a disservice. So I would be perfectly willing to entertain proposals from students that we keep open twenty-four hours a day. Some libraries have done it very successfully.

You do not think that such a schedule depreciates the quality of library service which a university has to offer?

I doubt if the hard facts of budgeting will enable us to put on qualified information crews around the clock, but I do not think that it is the information services that these people want so much as the book collection itself. It seems to me that this is a legitimate desire. When you stop to think of the value of the collection as a capital asset of the university, it seems to me that it is fantastic. If you took the Emory book collection back to the beginning and said that you invested a certain number of dollars in it each year from that time until now, and then appreciated the value of the expenditures year after year up to now, and then added to it the contributed value of your services in acquiring and cataloging from the beginning until now, and if you took the cost of living and inflation into account also, it would probably turn out that in your library you had an asset of the university worth perhaps $20 million. If you then say that for the lack of $20,000 a year you are going to deny students for one-third of the twenty-four-hour day access to this $20 million asset, it seems to me that it would be a misplacement of funds. If the students want it, I think that your university ought to find the $20,000 necessary to keep that asset available to them around the clock.

If you had to weigh this demand against other needs of the library, would you still feel the same way? Money to expand and maintain the present book stock, for example?

I feel quite certain that I would. On a $1 million book budget, $20,000 represents a 2 percent increase. I believe that public services would improve more than 2 percent if that $20,000 went instead into night staff.

What would you regard as necessary to staff a library under those circumstances?

If you have a modern library building with a single exit, it seems to me that you would need one person at the exit, someone at the circulation desk who would render at least basic circulation services, and then two additional men just roaming the building. So you might say that you need three people and a student assistant.

At one time loyalty to one's institution was a fairly common trait among administrators, faculty, and librarians. In recent years this bond seems to have been weakened. Do you agree with this, and if so, how do you explain it?

Yes, I think what you say is true. I think that we no longer have people, as we once had, whose strong allegiance is to an institution. In fact, I heard someone suggest that historically the faculty had the American Association of University Professors and tenure to protect itself from a capricious administration, but now it is coming rapidly to a point where the university needs some kind of reverse tenure to protect itself from the capricious faculty member. Isn't this, however, simply the inevitable result of full employment? There is no such thing as unemployment. Indeed, there is a great shortage of people in all industries. I heard this shortage attributed to something interesting recently. Maybe this is something everybody else has thought of except me, but it came as an interesting proposal to me at any rate. Why are there more jobs right now than there are people? The reason suggested was that the most marketable people today are the depression generation when few babies were born. But this generation is being called upon now to serve a rapidly growing population of people who were born during the baby boom of World War II and immediately afterwards. So there is really a shortage of people coming of age to serve this vastly increasing population. The shortage of trained people exists in librarianship as well as in all other fields. This means that a person does not have to accept gaff from anybody. He can always go some place else and make more money than he is making where he is now. I doubt that this has ever before been true to the degree that it is true today. In order to fill a position, you have to find someone who is employed and offer him more money and more perquisites than he is getting now to make your job attractive.

Doesn't this situation produce some unhappy results? Faculties which become deeply involved in the determination of their status and careers, even the support of their own discipline as against the good of the institution as a whole, become obsessed with matters which have a strong personal flavor? I sense that this virus may be beginning to infect the library staff.

Maybe it is the way you have described. I am not sure, however, that it is all bad. What we need is to develop people with a stronger sense of professional responsibility than we have done in the past. In the past, librarians have often had a greater sense of responsibility to an institution; now it is more to their profession. I am not sure that this represents a more selfish concern for one's personal career, although I am sure there are always people who move where they can do the best for themselves. If we are developing people with a stronger professional sense than we once did—and I believe we are doing this—then it may be that they will feel obliged to move from one job to another because their professional contribution will be greater in the new position than in the old, and I am not sure that this is necessarily bad. I think we have all seen people who could have made a greater professional contribution by moving than they were able to make in the institution with which they chose to remain aligned. Maybe, therefore, it is healthy that people are now making a stronger tie to the profession.

What do you consider to be the two or three major problems confronting academic librarians today?

I suppose one of the things which I find myself most frequently waking up with a start about is the need for continuing education. Things are changing so fast that the old-fashioned kind of librarian simply no longer exists—the situation where you got your degree and took a job for forty years. If a librarian doesn't upgrade his ability to serve at least every five years, he's out-of-date; he's obsolete. He's not going to make a contribution. This is one of the things that is challenging librarians today, and we must attack it on several fronts. Our library schools are attempting to set up workshops, but the need for upgrading the librarian's education should also challenge the head librarian. It seems to me that library management has to do much more than it has done in the past in the area of continuing education, furnishing opportunity for professional growth. We have not been as vigorous in furnishing these opportunities as we must be in the future.

We are also likely to see involvement of more librarians in library management. I recently heard someone maligning the idea of the director of libraries being chosen by the staff. I am not sure that this would be a bad thing. I like to think that the staff member is going to take the best interests of the library to heart. This means he will urge the appointment of the best person for the directorship. Just as faculty appoint their own deans and departmental chairman, I think that we might follow a similar procedure in library management and have department and division heads, at least, nominated by staff. Widespread involvement and participation of professional staff in decision making at all levels will strengthen greatly the library's ability to render service of the best quality.

Do you see librarians becoming more involved in the total educational purpose of the university as a result of greater participation in library management and in their own welfare?

Yes, I do. There are some librarians who chose librarianship so that they would not have to get involved. They went into

it by default. They started out as something else and then decided they did not want to go into an assertive profession and
therefore chose librarianship as a passive profession. This kind
of person is fulfilling a less and less viable role in academic
librarianship. It seems to me that a professional staff member
is going increasingly to have to work as a doctor does in a
hospital—participating in the decision-making that the hospital
has to face. I do not believe a director of libraries should tell a
professional librarian how to do his job anymore than a hospital
director tells a surgeon how to operate. The surgeon is the expert
and the catalog librarian is the expert.

William P. Kellam

PORTER KELLAM has brought to librarianship a broad background in both teaching and university library work. For two years he served as a teacher and principal in the schools of North Carolina following his graduation from Duke University (B.A., 1926; M.A., 1929). Switching to librarianship, he prepared himself by a period of apprentice training in various positions in the Duke and University of North Carolina libraries and by completing his studies for a degree in library science at Emory University. Before assuming his present position as Director of the University of Georgia Libraries, he held the head library position at what was then called North Carolina State College at Raleigh, N. C., West Virginia University, and the University of South Carolina. During the period of 1952 to 1961 he edited the *Southeastern Librarian.* The moral of his career is, one might suppose, that success as a librarian comes from a long apprenticeship of academic and administrative experience. This may be true, but Porter Kellam's closest colleagues will say that at least a part of his success is due to his admirable character—warm hearted, practical yet idealistic, refreshingly and generously unassuming.

Recently you have had a tremendous upsurge in support for your university library. It is said that a good librarian ad-

*ministrator cannot get this kind of financial backing unless he
has a broad base of support on the campus. Can you attribute
your success in any way to the effort of an active library
committee?*

No, I do not think that I can. Of course, the committee has
supported our requests. It may have had some influence, but
I think the main reason for our advance is an enlightened university administration which realized that you must have a good
library, a great library, in order to have a great university. It
has shown a willingness to put up the money, even sacrificing
other academic needs in order to accomplish this.

What circumstances brought about this advance?

We started moving forward when Dr. George Parthemos
was made vice-president of the University of Georgia. He had
formerly been head of the Department of Political Science and
was, I suppose, one of our best teachers here on the campus.
He required students to use the library a great deal and he
used it himself extensively. Up until that time, the library had
not had a really strong advocate among the top echelon of administrators. He and I had many talks about the library. When
he first went into office, he appointed a number of committees,
"task forces" he called them, and one of these was to concern
itself with library matters quite separate from the regular library
committee. This task force had several meetings, agreed on what
should be done, but unfortunately wanted the director of libraries to do all the work. So I prepared a rather lengthy statement of needs. I took the University of Virginia, Duke, University of North Carolina, University of Florida, Louisiana
State University, and the University of Georgia and went
back thirty years, using the statistics put out annually by Louisiana
State University for total library expenditures, staff, and book
expenditures, and came up with a document showing that we
had been and were far below the others. This report was presented to the committee, accepted, and in a somewhat shorter
version, incorporated in my annual report for 1965-1966. The
report appeared just before Dr. Fred Davison left the University
of Georgia to become assistant chancellor of the University
System. He told me that he was very much interested in the
report and that he was taking it with him and would see what
could be done to improve the situation. Something was done

about it. During the next year our book funds, staff, and everything else were more than doubled. Our former president had started a move in that direction, but Dr. Davison, who returned to the University of Georgia to become its president, and Dr. Parthemos deserve most of the credit for the increased on-going support.

I am not sure how many members there are in the Association of Research Libraries, perhaps eighty or more. When you made your initial comparison you must have been near the bottom of the list. Where do you stand now?

We were not a member of the Association of Research Libraries at that time, but if a comparison had been made, we would have been far down the list. In 1967-1968 we ranked seventh in expenditures for books, journals, and binding.

Well that's a remarkable record. And apparently it took place in the short span of two or three years because strong administrative backing was forthcoming?

Yes, it takes an administration willing to back the library with more than lip service to accomplish a growth of this kind.

I have found the library committee helpful as a sounding board, as a debating place, and as an interpreter, but not helpful in getting financial support for the library. I would judge that this might be generally the case. What is your opinion?

I think what you say is true. I have used committee members in various ways and they have always come to my support. They have served as a liaison between the library and the faculty. But as I pointed out earlier, the thing that triggered our financial advance was the appointment of a special task force, quite apart from the library committee, which had the full support of the administration. The library committee has been most helpful in questions relating to departmental libraries, duplication of library materials, and the like. We have not used the library committee here as much as we could have, but it has helped whenever it has been called upon. The committee members are busy people. They act in an advisory capacity and have not tried too much to take the bit in their teeth, but they have helped when needed.

Do you think the library committee can or should initiate support among the faculty for the library?

I think that the librarian should give the library committee leadership. Being advisory, they cannot take the initiative. I have found them very willing to be helpful and cooperative when called upon. Recently, I have asked the library committee to make certain studies. We have a request from faculty members to circulate journals, particularly among scientific departments. I brought this matter before the library committee to discuss what the cost of such a service would be and to see how many departments would want it. We sent out a brief questionnaire and are now compiling the data. I shall present it to the committee at a future meeting.

Will this mean duplicating all journals that are circulated?

A certain number of them. Some of the departments are quite enthusiastic, and it will be probably a wise expenditure of money to duplicate as much as is needed to provide this service.

Did you initiate the idea?

I initiated it with the committee, but one of the faculty members first wrote to see if such a service could be provided. In fact, it originated with a new man who came here from Iowa State University.

You are one of the few university libraries in the Southeast which makes extensive use of "blanket" orders in current book buying. With whom do you have blanket order contracts and for what countries and types of materials?

We have blanket order contracts with two firms: Richard Abel & Company, Inc., and Otto Harrassowitz. Abel furnishes us with one copy of scholarly publications in English issued by publishers in Australia, Canada, Great Britain, Japan, New Zealand, South Africa, the United States, and Western Europe. Harrassowitz supplies scholarly books issued in East and West Germany, Austria, and the German portion of Switzerland.

Certain types of materials are excluded from both plans. They are juveniles, textbooks, periodicals, syllabi, classroom or laboratory manuals, clinical medicine, fiction, reprints, law, denominational and evangelical works, travel and history books consisting mainly of pictures and which are popular in treatment, and engineering (except for agricultural).

What are the terms of your agreement with the dealers?

No book costing more than $50 will be supplied without confirmation. All books are sent on approval and any book received may be returned for full credit if it is found to be undesirable. Discounts average about 10 percent. Return postage on books, which the library pays, may be heavy if there are many returns. Extra benefits in service account for the low discount. These benefits are, first, the right to return any book for any reason whatever; second, a standing invitation to call the dealer collect when any problem arises; and third, provision by the dealer of a set of multiple forms for each book, made to the library's specifications.

Do your acquisitions staff or faculty members make any systematic effort to screen incoming material with a view to weeding out and returning titles which you do not want?

Yes. The acquisitions librarian examines all volumes and selects those to be returned. Other staff members will examine them when larger quarters are available.

Do you feel that you are getting the kind of coverage of important research materials which you need through the blanket order plan? Do you have to supplement what the dealer sends by a systematic study of trade bibliography?

Yes, we believe we get satisfactory coverage. We make no systematic effort to check trade bibliographies but we keep a sharp watch for the publications of societies, associations, and small publishers which are not included in the standing order contracts.

Has the blanket order plan eliminated the need for allocating book funds or do you still need departmental allocations to encourage faculty selection of retrospective material?

We have reduced departmental allocations but have not eliminated any of them. Some libraries with standing orders have eliminated book allocations to departments but we are not ready to do this yet. I feel that faculty interest in book selection should be maintained as long as it is possible to do so.

Another recent trend in library acquisitions is the growing use of library bibliographers in selection. A good many libraries on the West Coast are following Indiana's lead in this direction. Do you make any provision for this service?

We have two bibliographers on our staff. For the most part they are devoting time to retrospective purchases, particularly in searching bibliographies and building up journal files. One of the weaknesses of faculty selection is that so often it is speculative. When they see something in a catalog, something advertised, something that meets a particular need at the moment, they go after it. But a library bibliographer can take a field in which the library is weak and build up a careful bibliography and place this in the hands of the order people who get the titles whenever they appear on a favorable market. This is to my way of thinking a sound way to build strong collections of retrospective materials.

Richard H. Logsdon

RICHARD LOGSDON was born in 1912 in Upper Sandusky, Ohio, and attended Western Reserve University where he received a B.A. degree in economics and a B.S. degree in library science. In 1942 he received his doctoral degree in library science from the University of Chicago. He has served successively as head of Adams State College (1934-1939), Madison College (1939-1943), the Department of Library Science of the University of Kentucky (1943-1945), chief librarian of the U.S. Office of Education (1945-1947), and as Assistant Director, Associate Director, and Director of Libraries at Columbia University since 1947. In July, 1969, he resigned his position at Columbia to become Dean of Libraries of the City University of New York, a publicly-supported, coeducational institution comprising fifteen colleges, a graduate center, and a medical school. These plain facts can be collected from any reference who's who or from the Library of Congress *Information Bulletin* for February 27, 1969.

Dr. Logsdon's extracurricular activities include notable periods of service as president of the New York Library Association and as a member of the New York Metropolitan Reference and Research Library Agency. He has served on the board of directors of the Association of Research Libraries and as chairman in 1964 when the Shared Cataloging Program was launched. Committee assignments included the Shared Cataloging Com-

mittee and Coordinating Committee for Slavic and East European
Library Resources (COCOSEERS). He is currently a member
of the Grolier Club. He has participated in surveys of college
and university libraries in Maine, New Hampshire, New York,
Pennsylvania, Maryland, Washington, D. C., Kansas, Michigan,
Puerto Rico, Canada, and Afghanistan. In his long service to the
ALA he served as a member of the Board of Education for Li-
brarianship (1946-1951), and as its chairman when the still-
current standards were developed, and as chairman of the Commission on a National Plan for Library Education (1962-1964).
Dr. Logsdon has co-authored two major survey reports, one of
the Columbia University Libraries (with C. Donald Cook and
Maurice F. Tauber) and another of McGill University (with
Stephen A. McCarthy). Irene Logsdon, a librarian in her own
right, has co-authored with her husband *Library Careers* (New
York, 1963), which makes for good reading for those who like
to believe that libraries have an important place in the scheme
of things.

This interview took place in New York on June 18, 1969.

---

*Although you will soon be leaving your library directorship
at Columbia for the deanship of libraries at City University, I
think it is appropriate that I should address some, if not most,
of my questions to your Columbia association. Separate undergraduate libraries today have become almost as common as reserve book rooms in the past. I believe Columbia has followed
a somewhat different pattern than most from the very beginning
by incorporating a college library in the same building as the
university library. How has this worked out?*

One of the first things I learned when I came here in 1947
was that Columbia was the first among private universities in
the East to provide a separate facility for undergraduates in its
central library building, in our case the Butler Library. It was
not, however, a self-contained unit. Rather, it was a basic collection of some 25,000 monograph titles, a small reference collection,
and facilities for reserve book service. It never really grew
much beyond that. So from the very first, Columbia College
students used it as a kind of home base and not as a unit intended
to take care of all their needs. The earlier (pre-Butler) name

"College Study" rather than the Columbia College Library persisted, even though the latter was painted on the door. In a study made in 1955, we found that less than half of library use by Columbia College undergraduates was furnished by this library.

Are there plans for expanding or changing the character of this library?

Yes, and dramatically. Butler and its associated facilities are to become a "University Library Center." We propose to separate resources and services as between those relating to research and those relating to instruction. It seemed clear to us that undergraduate libraries such as at Harvard, Michigan, and elsewhere were in fact something more than that.

So very early in Columbia's planning we established the concept of a separate library facility to serve the teaching function of the University without regard for the level of instruction. By providing for mass use in new quarters designed for the purpose, we hope to take undue pressure off the research collections. We are planning a facility of some two or three hundred thousand volumes, including heavily used periodical runs and nonprint materials which will provide a working collection for all of the teaching purposes of the University. University libraries are woefully behind in nonprint materials and facilities related to teaching compared with good high schools and colleges.

Graduate as well as undergraduate?

Both. We might even define our proposed teaching collection as books which are likely to be in demand by groups of students as opposed to books which might be used by the individual student.

A difficult division to make—in terms of collection, is it not?

Yes, but the teaching collection will be largely duplicate. Our more serious difficulty lies in placing proper limits on the proposed collection. We want it to be complete enough to satisfy most teaching needs in one stop so that students can predict in advance whether or not they will need to consult the research collections. This is important because, as you well know, the very completeness of the research collections makes it difficult for undergraduates to use library facilities for teaching purposes. The dependable teaching titles are shelved along with those which are brought together for quite different purposes; they are imbedded, so to speak, in a mass of recondite material. We must also keep in mind the necessity of providing separate facilities for rare books and manuscripts. In the years ahead, we believe that the deteriorating paper problem will oblige university libraries to make available an increasing proportion of their research collections only under surveillance use in rare book libraries.

Do you plan to house this teaching library as a separate library unit?

As mentioned earlier, Butler is to be a University Library Center. We are recommending an extension and renovation of that building. The instructional library will be in new and separate quarters. I could go on at some length but perhaps this answers your question.

I believe you mentioned duplicating titles in the instructional library. On what grounds is this defensible?

The materials will be essentially duplicated and semi-expendable. A research collection by definition aims at completeness. It contains the instructional materials as well as the more obscure and little-known items. If the standard works in an instructional collection were removed from the research collection, we would no longer have a research library. In any case, the demand for the kind of materials we plan for the teaching collection is so great that duplication is necessary.

Will you find it difficult to convince a faculty and administration that the library is justified in putting the kind of money that will be needed for this project into what essentially amounts to duplication? Do not misunderstand me! I am all for the idea, but the question has been raised before.

No! Or at least I hope not. We are more likely to have difficulty convincing the faculty, who, in spite of current difficulties, still tend to be graduate-student and research oriented. They will not want to give up their separate library facilities for graduate instruction—what we call laboratory collections, even though they are heavily used by undergraduates. Many of the faculty feel that it is desirable to have special quarters for their doctoral and better master students. They do not want to have them mix with undergraduates. We hope to meet their objections by accepting a period of transition, retaining highly selective core collections for graduate students until the new facility can demonstrate its effectiveness for both purposes.

Were there petitions or complaints from undergraduates about library services during the period of student dissension on the campus?

Not really. Everyone was so completely occupied by the major issues (or at least by the incredible turmoil created on campus by recurring mob-like situations) that we were left alone at first and then singled out for "protection." At the height of the crises in May, 1968, for example, I was told that one of the dissident student leaders walked into a strategy meeting claiming 150 supporters, and hence 3 votes on the Council, to move that the libraries be declared neutral territory and that they be permitted to operate without interference. This we did essentially throughout the period.

Are students represented in the formulation of library policies and regulations?

Not directly, that is, up until this past year. Periodically we have found ways of consulting students. Our student assistants have always served as an ear to the ground for us in matters relating to student needs.

What plans are there now for student participation?

In view of Columbia's size, we feel that efforts to secure student participation need to move on many fronts. For example, take the School of Library Service. The Faculty Library Committee has been reactivated and now includes students in its membership. We have also created a new University-wide committee on library services with joint representation from faculty, students, and members of the library staff. Whereas the central University Library Committee includes only the Director of Libraries and six faculty representatives, the new committee has five members from the library staff, ten or more faculty members, and an equal number of students. This may now change since a newly created University Senate provides for a Library Committee which will include members of the Senate, faculty members outside the Senate, students, and librarians.

How has the faculty library committee been structured in the past?

Since 1951, it has been a creature of the University Council, which was the nearest thing we had to a University Senate in the past. More recently we endeavored to bring the library a little closer to the decision-making leadership by drawing directly on the educational policy committees of the separate faculties. Instead of having the University Council elect this library committee, we asked each of six Committees on Instruction to name one of their members to the University Library Committee. For example, we had a faculty member from philosophy representing the humanities, from political science representing the social sciences, and so forth. The Vice-President has served as chairman, the Dean of the Graduate Faculties as vice-chairman, and the Director of Libraries as secretary.

When you, Dr. Tauber, and Mr. Cook prepared your survey of the Columbia University Libraries some ten years ago you stressed the importance of strong faculty participation in the selection of materials for the University Library. You even made recommendations as to how faculty selection might be extended and improved. Is it true that since that survey was made the actual selection of materials for university libraries has largely shifted from the faculty to the library staff and that university libraries now show less concern for selection and more for comprehensiveness of coverage?

No question about this at Columbia, and I suspect that the actual practice in most university libraries today would show that librarians are assuming a much larger responsibility for selection than ever before. By and large, the faculty expect the library to have most of the material they need. I would say that the acquisition of 75 to 90 percent of the material coming into the university library at Columbia today is initiated by the library staff. This is particularly true in the area studies programs, where the specialist bibliographers initiate most of the orders. We also lean heavily on the librarians in charge of our different subject libraries to carry the responsibility of selection. We try to get double or triple duty out of subject bibliographers. In some cases, they are in charge of collections, assist readers in using the materials, and have a major responsibility for book selection.

In your distinguished career you have been closely associated with cooperative movements. In New York State you have a state-wide cooperative program known as the 3R program. How is this cooperative effort organized and financed and how would you evaluate its accomplishment?

The whole idea of the 3R's* program is to get more effective use of existing resources, to break down the barriers to co-operation, to pool resources in an orderly fashion, and to get more mileage out of the strong collections in the state. Concurrently, looking down the road, we are interested in finding ways to enlist the state in helping libraries to strengthen their research collections. To be more specific, take the example of SUNY, the State University of New York, which is a whole new system of higher education in this state. You might say that with few exceptions the libraries of SUNY are starting from scratch; but along with them you have a number of older institutions such as Columbia, Cornell, Fordham, New York University, and the New York Public with rich collections but insufficient funds to sustain services to their regular clientele, to say nothing of extending their services to others. The 3R's program offers a way to make collections at Columbia or Cornell, for example, available to persons outside these institutions, and in return to reimburse them as a means of sustaining their strength. To be more specific, the East Asian collections at Columbia are growing rapidly from the University's appropriations with some federal help; but we need at least another hundred thousand dollars a year to do the job properly. With that level of financing by the state, we could backstop East Asian study programs wherever they existed in the state. I might mention that the 3R's program is organized through regional councils. In New York City, for example, we have the New York Metropolitan Reference and Research Agency (METRO), separately incorporated, which is one of them.

So far as evaluation is concerned, I think about all that can be said is that we now have the structure, and, on an *ad hoc* basis, are fielding a number of different projects. We perhaps 10 percent down the road to our potential.

What are some of the specific projects which METRO is sponsoring?

---

*Reference and Research Library Resources Program (New York State).

SHARES comes to mind first because I have been drafted to serve as Chairman of the Advisory Committee for the Project. The acronym stands for Shared Acquisitions and Retention System. I could talk for an hour on this program and not do it justice. The concept back of it has dominated discussions of regional and national library cooperation for at least my period of service at Columbia. It incorporates the whole philosophy of cooperative acquisition, cooperative storage of lesser used materials, and cooperative access. After careful review of past and present thinking and the help of two consultants, Russell Shank in a Study of Science Information facilities and Hendrik Edelman in a study of cooperative storage, we have reached four major conclusions: (1) that the Research Libraries of the New York Public Library might take responsibility for the retention of basic monographs and serial publications not needed in other libraries in the area; (2) that responsibility for collecting and retaining such categories of material as college catalogs, technical reports, and doctoral dissertations might be placed with one or another member of METRO; (3) that the Library of Congress or the Center for Research Libraries might be expected to do the same for materials needed only in one place for the country as a whole; and (4) that responsibility for the acquisition of major research items (e.g., large microfacsimile projects where one copy in the area would be sufficient) might be assigned to one of the METRO member libraries for the use of all. We shall have to see what comes of this proposal. If it doesn't work out in practice, we shall have to revise our ideas of the possible benefits of cooperation.

Are you securing state support for the 3R program?

Yes, but in modest amounts. Each council receives a block grant for a small secretariat and may apply for project money. The state also subsidizes NYSILL, the interlibrary loan project which was started in 1967. NYSILL is in effect a network with backstop libraries receiving a standby grant ($10,000), plus payments for requests processed, and additionally for those filled. Columbia, for example, backstops the network for fifteen different subject fields in which we have particular strength.

Many cooperative programs have started out with great promise and then folded along the way. Actually, there are very few cooperative programs which embrace cooperation both at the acquisition and lending level which have proved worthwhile. Do you think the New York cooperative program is strongly enough based to go on to greater accomplishment?

In METRO we are determined that we are going to find a way to identify the categories of materials and the kinds of materials and collections which, if reasonably complete and comprehensive in one place, can meet the total needs of the metropolitan area. We are determined that in such things as college catalogs, technical reports, PL 480* materials, and the like we are going to find the way to have one library or another take the full responsibility for the area so that everyone else can be relieved of the responsibility, or at least can pattern its local program with the realization that their readers have access to a METRO-sponsored collection of strength. Nor are we forgetting the needs of the more general reader. Only recently a special committee of METRO dealt with the possibilities of bringing together in one place a complete collection of all H. W. Wilson indexed materials, including the *Essay & General Literature* indexes.

Similarily, we are determined to correlate the work and services of all major libraries in the area and in the state. SUNY and CUNY (City University of New York), for example, cannot at this stage duplicate the retrospective holdings of the New York Public Library, nor of two or three of the other large research libraries in the area. We must create a viable system of joint collections development and use with proper subsidies to backstopping institutions.

You are also a member of a coordinating committee for Slavic and East European library resources. What and for whom are you coordinating these resources?

You are referring, I think, to a project of the Association of Research Libraries which began some years ago as COCOSEERS. The work of this earlier organization, since disbanded, led to the recent Ford Foundation grant to establish a Slavic Bibliographic and Documentation Center in Washington.

---

*Public Law 480. The Agricultural Trade Development and Assistance Act of 1954 authorizes the use of surplus U.S. owned local currencies, acquired in many countries by the sale of surplus agricultural commodities, for the purchase by the Library of Congress of library materials for distribution to American research libraries.

One of the objectives is to achieve more effective bibliographical control of material which is not generally found in the national bibliographies. In the earlier stages, at least, I think the emphasis will be on the acquisition and cataloging of the unusual and on what frequently appears to be ephemeral material. Although I am not working with this group now, I hope that the Center will be able to tap the unusual input of those universities which have aggressive acquisition programs in support of Slavic studies and by one device or another make this material available first bibliographically and secondly through republication in microform or hard copy. We must somehow find ways to pool our know-how more effectively. Incidentally, few people realize, I think, that COCOSEERS was the breeding ground for the Shared Cataloging Program. The dilemma of backlogs and the slow processing of Slavic materials which was discussed freely with our academic colleagues encouraged me in 1964 to recommend that the Association of Research Libraries go all out for what Ralph Ellsworth and others had been recommending for a generation—a massive attack on the problem of producing centrally and quickly at the Library of Congress the catalog information needed by research libraries. We set a goal of 250,000 monograph titles a year. The figure is already in excess of 200,000, almost doubling in the four years the program has been in operation.

You have also been involved in cooperation in the field of automation studies, I believe—in a cooperative study project of Columbia, Stanford, and the University of Chicago. What has developed from this joint project so far?

Very simply, the three universities received grants to do the necessary analytical work and to design computer-based systems for various aspects of their internal library operations. Chicago received a National Science Foundation grant, Stanford an HEW grant, and Columbia followed with a National Science Foundation grant. The National Science Foundation hoped to have the local work in research and development in these separate universities shared more effectively and efficiently among the three—and more importantly, with the profession generally. This led to a fourth grant to finance the collaboration, which because of availability of office space came to Columbia with my serving as project director. Columbia joined with Stanford and Chicago in sponsoring a conference on collaborative library systems development in October, 1968. The proceedings have been published recently by the Stanford University Libraries. The three libraries are concentrating on very close cooperation among the technical staff members of these three institutions. Each one has its senior systems person who meets with the others monthly. Although the results are not as visible as one might wish, they are being made available through regular reports to the National Science Foundation and through the participation of the principal investigators in a variety of conferences, workshops, and publications.

Are the libraries working on different aspects of technical processes?

Chicago has concentrated on cataloging, Columbia more on the acquisition side, while Stanford is in a position to interrelate its library development work in the technical services with spires, a physics-oriented research project dealing with information handling. Columbia has also been working on the design of a computer-controlled reserve bank system and the development of a circulation control system. The grant has made possible very close cooperation of the technical personnel involved.

For some years now Columbia has had an active Friends of the Library organization. I am interested to learn what makes a group of friends a really effective supporter of the library instead of being merely a group of well-wishers.

We started out in New York City in a highly competitive climate with a very simple idea, namely, that there were in the city many persons, some with Columbia affiliation but others not, who were interested in books, manuscripts, book collecting, and libraries, and that among these were those who might enjoy some sort of formal association with the University through their interest in books. Actually, we reactivated in 1951 an association which was started by Dr. C. C. Williamson in the early 1940's. Our Friends' group serves as a bridge between the University and book-minded members of the New York community. We took the long view that the organization might generate interest in Columbia and bequests, as well as annual gifts of books and money. I think all these hopes have been realized in one form or another. The organization takes a fair amount of library time, but the Friends' contributions finance fully the cost of publishing *Library Columns*. This publication is very well received throughout the country. It not only helps to keep us in touch with one another but it serves as a continuous reporting medium for library gifts and activities. It has helped to generate tremendous book gifts which I think would probably amount to more than a million and a half dollars since 1951.

Does the library assume the responsibility for editing Library Columns *or is this done outside by members of the Friends' organization?*

A combination—Charlie Mixer, our Assistant Director of Libraries, is an experienced editor and has a particular interest in the *Columns*. He also serves as secretary of the Friends. He works closely with the editor, Dr. Dallas Pratt, who is a graduate of Columbia's College of Physicians and Surgeons and a member of the Council of Friends. Another of our graduates, also a physician, is chairman of the Friends' group. I imagine he gives a day or more each month to the organization. We have a board of twenty-one members which meets every two or three months. We sponsor four programs a year, frequently relating them to the announcement of major gifts. The existence of the Friends of the Library organization has provided an excellent platform for appropriate acknowledgment of gifts from alumni or others who are not members of the organization. Last year, for example, when we received the papers of a distinguished publishing house, the Friends joined with the publishing firm in building a program around this gift. This occasion enabled us to bring to the campus many people, including alumni, who had little previous association with Columbia, at least since student days. They were much interested in the publishing firm or were formerly connected with it. We use the Friends to extend our influence and contacts in the community. Some of the Friends have been working with us for many years and their interest has resulted in gifts of collections and bequests.

Another special feature of your operations is of general interest to urban university libraries. These libraries are always under pressure to assist noncollege persons. I believe you are one of the institutions that charges a fee to outside library users. How does this work?

In 1939, Dr. C. C. Williamson, who was unquestionably one of the great librarians of his time, called attention in his annual report to the fact that too many people were pressing Columbia for use of its collections and in so doing were destroying the library's capability for meeting Columbia's needs. He recommended a fee to outsiders, I believe, of only five dollars a semester. The faculty reacted strongly and of course negatively, even though Dr. Williamson gave them a year's advance notice of the intention to charge a fee. As a result, numerous exceptions developed to the point that few people paid the fee, modest as it was. A few years later, in 1951, we came back to the idea of a fee for "use of university facilities" including the library; more recently we have called it, forthrightly, a library fee, which is $25 per month or $200 per year. Actually all through the years Columbia has offered extensive services without fee. All alumni, for example, have reading privileges. Similarly, any person engaged in scholarly work, comparable to that typical of a university community, is given access to manuscript collections and other materials available only at Columbia. And of course all material is available under normal interlibrary loan procedures.

Do you have any method of checking outside use to determine if the fee is being enforced?

In recent years, we have made periodic checks as readers come into the library. On Sundays, for example, we check identification on the way into Butler Library because this is a time when many students from other institutions as well as persons from the outside come to use the library. Access to the central stacks is checked continuously by a uniformed guard.

Tell me about your new position as University Dean of Libraries of the City University of New York.

I am to represent the chancellor's office on library matters throughout the City University system. In essence, the position is like that of a vice-chancellor for library planning and development, although this title is not used. This involves the same relationship to the colleges and other librarians in the system as the chancellor has to the college presidents and other local officers. It is not, at this time, a line position, although some would have it be. The librarians report directly to their respective deans and presidents. It is a new position and we do not really know yet what it should finally be. I have some ideas and will be presenting them to the Council of Chief Librarians of the eighteen different institutions. We shall work out the priorities together.

What are some of the ideas you propose to consider with the Council?

A matter of immediate concern relates to services to be provided to City University by the New York Public Library. In the constraints of this year's budget, for example, the New York Public Library was faced with the necessity of reducing services substantially. In the end, City University's budget was increased by a half-million dollars to assist the New York Public Library in the restoration of services. This was to produce another half-million from state funds, all of which would be funneled to the public library through City University. One of my first assignments is to work with City University committees and the New York Public Library in specifying what special services ought to be provided from this million dollars.

There is a long list of more specific projects including co-ordination of acquisitions policies, union catalogs, and proper formulae, if any, for budgeting and for planning new library buildings. I will spend the first two months going through the documents anticipating meetings with the librarians individually and as a council this coming fall. It will be a vast change from Columbia but I trust no less exciting and satisfying. It's where the action is going to be in the years ahead if we are to solve our urban problems.

John G. Lorenz

THE Library of Congress is not only the most distinguished scholarly library in the United States but also a national institution. As such it is of vital interest and concern to university librarians. If Lyman H. Butterfield can write "every working scholar in the United States may be said to have at least two libraries at his service—that of his own institution, and the Library of Congress," it seems altogether fitting to hear from L.C.'s deputy landlord in a collection of interviews with university librarians.

John Lorenz was born in New York City in 1915; his father, a postal supervisor, sent him to the City College of New York where he graduated with a bachelor in science degree in 1939. In 1940 he obtained the B.S. degree from Columbia University's School of Library Service and, while serving as assistant librarian of the Michigan State Library, an M.S. in public administration (1952) from Michigan State University.

Mr. Lorenz first became widely known among librarians when he became associated with the Library Services Branch of the U.S. Office of Education. During the period of 1958 to 1963, he made important contributions as chief of the Branch to the pioneer development of federal legislation in aid of libraries. He participated in a large number of regional conferences on federal aid and served as liaison with state library agencies and with library administrators. As director of the Library Services Branch, he administered the library grant program. In May, 1964, after the passage of the expanded Library Service and Construction Act, he was named director of the Division of Library Services and Educational Facilities.

In view of his experience as library administrator and as a government figure on friendly terms with officials of the U.S. Office of Education and librarians throughout the country, it is not surprising that Mr. Lorenz was selected for the number two post in the Library of Congress. Named Deputy Librarian in October, 1965, Mr. Lorenz brought to his new position not only the measure of his cumulative experience as a successful administrator, but also shrewd judgment and a resolute thoroughness in his approach to planning and administration.

Mr. Lorenz was interviewed in Atlanta on March 30, 1969.

Can you talk for a moment about just what the Deputy Librarian of Congress does?

I am the Librarian's deputy in the full sense of the word. I take his place in anything that needs to be done for which he is not available, including testifying before congressional committees, welcoming visitors to the library, and so forth. More specifically, I have a direct responsibility for the auditing operation in the library and for the Information Systems Office which heads up our total automation effort. Generally speaking, I represent the Librarian in anything he wishes me to do.

Do your responsibilities encompass the administration of a large staff which reports directly to you?

The Information Systems Office has a total staff of about sixty people. This represents tremendous growth in the few years since its beginning with only a small staff of five. The auditing function also reports directly to the Deputy Librarian. So you might say that I have direct responsibility for these two functions; all other functions I share with the Librarian.

If the head of reference had a major problem in his department, would he seek your direction in this matter?

If it was in the area of budget, personnel, or something that could be handled administratively, he might very well discuss it with me. On the other hand, if it were a major question of policy, he would review it with the Librarian. Each department director does have weekly sessions with the Librarian. The Librarian is a very active administrator and has a continuing contact with the major departments of the library.

Obviously, you have responsibilities of administration which are more varied and complex than most of us have in the university library field. When and where did you develop the principles of management which you now use in your position?

In terms of experience, I would say principally at the Michigan State Library where as Assistant State Librarian I had the kind of administrative-budgetary-personnel responsibility which I have as Deputy Librarian of Congress. While at the Michigan State Library, I discovered that experience alone was not sufficient. I took the time to attend Michigan State summers and evenings and acquired a master's degree in public administration. So that added to my experience and training as well. Then, of course, when I left the Michigan State Library for the Office of Education in Washington, D. C., my position there once again presented a tremendous administrative challenge. When I arrived in Washington, the Library Services Branch had a small staff of five people headed by Ralph Dunbar and a total budget of approximately $200,000 a year. Ralph left within one year and I succeeded him as director of the Library Services Branch. You may remember that this was the time when the federal library grant program was just beginning. The Library Services Act started in 1957 with a grant of $2 million. My position afforded the experience of working with federal administrators at all levels, the immediate supervisors in the Office of the Commissioner, and the staff at the departmental level in the office of the General Council. I also worked with all state library agencies throughout the country, interpreting the legislation to each agency and reviewing state plans and programs. I might say that this was a real trial by fire because at the same time that I was getting all this under way, I had to recruit staff for the Washington office. We very quickly moved on from the very small Library Services Act to the Library Services and Construction Act, which opened up the program to urban as well as to rural areas and added the construction of public libraries as well. Then we moved on to school, college, and university library legislation; library research; and library training programs. This was a fascinating experience because we were working with officials in Washington, state librarians throughout the country, the ALA Washington office, and many others. All of this added to my sum total of experience and training for administrative work. You cannot underestimate the value of the personal contacts that you make over the years of service; these are still of great value to me in my work at the Library of Congress.

You mentioned that your training in public administration has been of great value to you in your administrative duties. Do you think that training in management principles should be incorporated into the education of librarians?

Yes, I do. To a large degree managers are born rather than made, but I think that the right kind of training and exposure to the principles of management and what it takes to develop good human relations can be taught to some degree; also it helps to reinforce what you might feel instinctively sometimes. I know that for a long time I have felt that good management is to a large degree human relations and I am very pleased to see that this is now coming out in the literature more and more.

When I was in library school, and I believe perhaps that this is still the pattern today in many administration courses, the chief thing we were taught about management was the making of an organization chart which broke the work of the library down into stratified functional groups. You suggest that more attention is being given to personal relationships today. How will this newer concept of organization affect the organization of libraries in the future?

Organization may change into smaller units of operation, with more staff participation in management decisions, particularly in determining the goals and objectives of the operation and evaluating progress toward these goals.

The report of the National Advisory Commission on Libraries recommends that the Library of Congress be given recognition as the national library of the United States. For many years, particularly under the provisions of the Higher Education Act of 1965, the Library of Congress has been serving as a national library. How would it serve differently from what it does now if Congress gave it the recognition recommended by the Commission?

That's a very good question and, as a matter of fact, we have been giving it some thought at the Library of Congress. I think our present position is that we are in fact performing more national library functions than any other national library in the world. We have undertaken already many huge responsibilities. You mentioned the "shared cataloguing" project under the Higher Education Act as one example of a major undertaking and huge responsibility. There are many others. Our hope and expectation for being formally and legally designated as the national library of the United States would be that this would result in greater recognition by the members of Congress that we need to be fully funded as a national library. It is true that in the past several years the funding of the Library of Congress has been generous and that our increases have been larger than they have ever been before. Nevertheless, if we are to continue to implement fully the programs which we have undertaken in shared cataloguing, and if we are to implement fully the responsibilities in automation that we are just beginning to enter upon, we shall need even greater funding than we have ever had before. We think that the designation must carry along with it the full recognition on the part of the members of the Congress that we need to be funded at this higher level in the future. In addition, we would hope that such a designation would remove any question about the need of the Library of Congress for the third building—the James Madison Memorial Library.

At present our major problem and our major handicap to program development is the need for space. We are absolutely up against it as far as expansion in the two buildings is concerned. We are already located in ten other areas throughout the region, extending from Baltimore to Alexandria, and all of this moving out of functions is done at great expense to efficiency of operation. So we would hope that the designation of the Library of Congress as a national library would help to move us toward the completion of a third building as rapidly as possible.

When you speak of a third building, I assume that numbers one and two are the Library of Congress and the Annex.

Yes, the James Madison is the third building, delayed last year for a full year because of the budget crisis. We didn't get the money for the final plans and specifications. Being set back a whole year on something like this is a very serious blow.

What is the status of the third building at present?

The money for the final plans and specifications is in the President's 1970 budget request. If this goes through this year, with all subsequent funding on schedule, it will be 1974 before we occupy the building. The pressure for space between now and 1974 will be terrific.

Wasn't there an effort some years ago to have the Library of Congress declared a national library?

Possibly so, but I am not familiar with it. Because of the many additions to its program which the present Librarian has achieved, the Library of Congress is doing many more things today than it has ever done before. There is one specific activity which we would probably add as a national library, what one might call a national bibliographic center. Such a center would enable us to develop and issue more bibliographic publications and also coordinate and bring together, or at least report on, all the other bibliographic efforts which are going on across the United States. This service has been broached from time to time as something that is obviously needed. I think that need still exists. I do not know whether, as a national library, we should assume the kinds of responsibilities the Association of Research Libraries is undertaking in its center for Chinese studies, Slavic studies, and the like, but it certainly would be a possibility. It is true that no matter where they are located or how they are administered, these centers use and rely heavily upon the resources of the Library of Congress.

Another recommendation in the report of the National Advisory Commission on Libraries relates to the establishment of a National Commission on Librarianship and Information Science as a continuing federal agency. Could this function be administered by the Division of Library Services in the Office of Education? Why have yet another Washington office?

I think the basis for the need for an overarching commission on libraries and information science is to try to coordinate all of the resources being made available to libraries and information science today. Even though the major portion of those resources is being funneled through the Division of Library Services Programs in the Office of Education, there are many other sources of funding which are of substantial importance such as the National Agricultural Library, the National Library of Medicine, the Library of Congress, the library programs sponsored by the National Science Foundation, all the other libraries in the whole hierarchy of federal agencies, and efforts such as those which are now being carried on in the office of the President through the Committee on Scientific and Technical Information. At the state level there are many research institutes and programs—for example, think of what is being done in the state of New York in developing the 3R system. There is no one body that embraces all of these interests and resources so that one is really forced, I think, to support the kind of overarching agency that can encompass all of the developments that are going on and try to coordinate the planning for the future. This is the only way I see to rationalize all the efforts that are being made, and the larger efforts that are going to be made in the future, in order to eliminate as much duplication as possible.

The only kind of body that I can see doing this is a national commission for libraries and information science which will bring together the resources in the legislative branch, represented by the Library of Congress, all of the resources of the executive branch, all of the resources that are available at the state levels, and perhaps most important, all the efforts that are being made in terms of science information on the one hand and all the developments that we know are needed in the fields of the humanities and social sciences on the other. It would also bring together efforts of both public and private agencies. I think it is this kind of national commission, with high visibility and people of real prestige supported by a small but very capable staff, that is needed. Only then will you have people who will be looked to for overall leadership. Going back to your original question, I think we have to admit that in its present organization and location, the Division for Library Services, even though it has progressed substantially in the Office of Education, still doesn't have the kind of legal responsibility, administrative placement, and power that is needed for the job.

Is the name of the proposed continuing agency, National Commission on Libraries and Information Science, suggestive of a split in what up to now we have thought of as librarianship?

No, I do not think so. I would hope that it would not develop this way. I think the reason for putting the two together is to show the close relationship between librarianship and information science rather than to represent the difference.

Do you believe that the recommendation for a national commission will be approved by Congress?

Yes. Within the last two weeks Congressman John Brademas of Indiana, a member of the House Committee on Education and Labor, has introduced a bill to establish such a commission. Many other key representatives on both sides of the aisle have introduced identical bills. On the Senate side, Senator Ralph Yarborough of Texas has introduced an identical bill. Hearings have been scheduled for April 15 and the Librarian of Congress is the key lead-off witness. There appears to be a lot of support for this measure and the prospects look good.

Through its grants to libraries, the federal government places a premium on library cooperation, as it should. Unfortunately, in academic libraries at least, the emphasis in fund awarding seems to be on the hardware of cooperation rather than on books and journals, which are the base of all cooperation. You cannot cooperate if you do not build and replenish your capital asset. This inequity is true of Title III and of several other programs. Why is this the case and can anything be done about it?

I hope the situation which you describe is a temporary misinterpretation of Title III of the Library Services and Construction Act, i.e., the interlibrary cooperation title. I was in the Office of Education when this title was written and I clearly recall that the title and its funding were to include all of the elements needed for cooperation, including the development of resources. It was only later that the regulations were drawn with this very narrow interpretation which emphasizes the new technology of librarianship rather than books and journals. The only explanation I can think of is that the initial funding was very limited and therefore it may have been felt necessary to put a narrow interpretation upon it. I agree that the present interpretation should be seriously challenged because I recognize the waste that is going on in manufacturing these artificial cooperative programs based on interconnections when there is nothing to interconnect. I can assure you that this was never the intention. Our feeling at the time it was developed was that this title could become the most important title in the entire Library Services and Construction Act program.

From what I have read of the Networks for Knowledge program (Title VIII) there is no money there for resources with which to cooperate—the emphasis once again seems to be on mechanical devices.

I think the present Networks for Knowledge title is so generally and loosely written that there is no telling what will develop out of it. I hope the regulations will make better sense out of what will and can be done than the words of the act itself.

As I understood it, one of the principal jobs of the Library Services Branch, at least in its early years, was the collection and dissemination of library statistics. In this effort, it has a very poor record. Beginning in 1959-1960 and for several years thereafter the Library Services Branch managed to get out detailed reports with some regularity. Then nothing appeared in 1964-1965 and 1965-1966. Only a preliminary report appeared in 1966-1967, and here we are in the academic year 1968-1969. What has happened and what can be done about it?

This has been one of the major defaults, I would say, of the Office of Education within the last four years. I think it is most regrettable. It is not only a failure in library statistics, but in practically all other educational statistics. It is now a very serious deficiency and a very serious lack. Going back, I would still maintain that the initial move to have the Office of Education assume the responsibility for college and university library statistics was a wise decision. As a result, the Office of Education was able to get out the official college and university library statistics in a more complete fashion than they had ever been published before. I think our returns were around 95 percent which was larger than the Association of College and Research Libraries had ever achieved. We were able to analyze these statistics more fully than ever before. It was these official statistics, indeed, that provided the ammunition for the inclusion of Title II* in the Higher Education Act of 1965. If we hadn't had these official data, I doubt if we ever would have been able to sell the college and university library resources title. All of us at that time expected that we could continue to build this statistics program with the staff we had right in the Library Services Branch. We had actually developed a statistical staff of about fifteen to twenty people who were collecting and publishing public, school, library education, and college and university library statistics in a quite competent fashion. Well, a new Commissioner of Education appeared on the horizon, a study was made to reorganize and improve the Office of Education, and one of the recommendations on which we had no opportunity to comment was to create a national educational statistical center to be staffed by picking up all the people who had been doing a very efficient job in the various units of the Office of Education and pooling them all in a single division. At that point the Library Services Branch lost control of the production of library statistics. The center was very poorly managed; the resources available were poorly assigned and poorly used, with the result that we had this debacle in the production of library statistics. The staff of the Library Services Branch complained, the ALA complained, and librarians generally complained. Finally, there are some encouraging signs that the seriousness of the present situation is being recognized and some attempts are being made to rectify the situation. Meanwhile, we have lost these very valuable years since 1966 in the production of needed library statistics.

Is the Center still the controlling unit?

The Center is still maintained but now a key person has been assigned the responsibility for library statistics.

How does the Division of Library Services now function with relation to statistics?

Purely in an advisory capacity. I do not know what the communication is between the Division and the Center. Fortunately, the man responsible for library statistics in the Center has had considerable experience with the library statistical program and has been one of our good cooperators over the years. The ques-

---

*The section that provides assistance to college libraries for the purchase of books and journals as well as grants for library training.

tion still remains as to whether he will be given the resources to carry out an adequate program.

You have had experience with the library services of UNESCO and IFLA (International Federation of Libraries). Most college and university librarians are not well acquainted with the library problems under discussion by these organizations, many of which have implications for the scholars who use libraries as well as for the libraries themselves. Can you fill in the picture so that we can get a better idea of what is going on in these organizations?

IFLA is an international library organization which has been limping along for quite a few years. It has served a useful purpose by providing an occasion where many of the leading librarians of the world could have contact with one another. By and large, the committees of IFLA have not been very productive, but certain progress has been made in international cataloging principles and other international standards. IFLA has provided an excellent means for the Library of Congress to communicate information on the shared cataloging program which in some respects has helped to regenerate the whole interest in international bibliographic cooperation. I really think that the personal contact afforded by the meetings, coupled with this new opportunity in the area of world-wide bibliographical control, may bring about a kind of rebirth of energy and interest in IFLA.

How is the United States represented?

The delegates are primarily those who, working through "sections" and "committees," have assignments and report at the annual meetings or conferences, as they are called. The principal means of being certified as an IFLA participant is through the ALA, which designates anyone who has official business through the sections or committees. Beyond that, individuals who are interested in participating as members of the larger group and are attending the general conferences may write to the Executive Board of the ALA and explain their interest and need. They can be certified if there are enough places. Each member association, of course, is limited to some degree by the number of people who may be certified. I would suppose that the ALA would like to see that the various divisions of the Association have at least one representative at these meetings.

You mentioned that some of the work was done through committees. What are some of these committees and have they worked successfully internationally?

There are committees on statistics, exchange of publications, uniform cataloging rules, library education, and others. There are also the sections which are organized by type of library such as the public libraries, parliamentary libraries, childrens' libraries, and the like. Of course, since IFLA is an international organization of library associations, there are representatives from Special Libraries, Music Libraries Association, and others at the annual meetings.

In what language are the meetings conducted?

The general sessions in the past few years have had simultaneous translation in English, French, and Russian. To some extent it depends upon the country in which the conference is held, but these are the general breakdowns. The committees and sections usually conduct their meetings in English with a summary translation in French or Russian if there is a particular demand. Summary proceedings are published in *Libri*, which also carries regular features and communications from IFLA.

In summing up what would you say were the major accomplishments of this international organization?

I think the major accomplishments are bibliographic cooperation and personal communication, which permit comparison of practice and experience, particularly in talks outside the framework of the formal conference meetings.

Do you think IFLA makes a contribution to good international relations?

Most definitely. For example, East-West differences tend to disappear. Even though we were invited to Moscow for 1969, an invitation which was declined in favor of Copenhagen after the occupation of Czechoslovakia, Moscow renewed its invitation to the association to meet there in 1970. When the IFLA executive board met recently in Washington, Madame Rudomino, Head of the All Union State Library of Foreign Literature,

Moscow, came to Washington and indicated that even though there are political differences among the members, the needs of the library profession must override political differences, bias, and prejudice. There was a very fine feeling of good will and cooperation.

Has language been a barrier for American representatives, and if it has, could anything be done by the representatives to bring this home to American librarians and librarians-in-training?

Lack of foreign language ability by Americans is sometimes a handicap. Generally, representatives of other countries are much better in English than we are in their language. I believe this point should be stressed and stated frequently by the ALA International Relations Office.

What about UNESCO in which you have also had experience? Has it concerned itself actively with libraries and have libraries contributed to the aims of UNESCO?

I think one can point to several good things that UNESCO has done in the library field, particularly in the developing countries. It is true that not all progress is in a straight line, but nevertheless there has been progress. For example, one of the finest library demonstrations ever staged in terms of reaching the people was one which took place under the auspices of UNESCO at Eastern Nigeria's Regional Central Library in Enugu, which was established as a pilot project. We had a seminar at Enugu in 1962 so that other countries of Africa south of the Sahara could see what this demonstration library had accomplished. I feel that the seminar made a considerable impact in the two and a half weeks it was in session. For the first time some of the younger participants saw what constituted good library service.

You say that not all progress is in a straight line. Do you care to say something more about this?

Well, wonderful as the Enugu seminar and demonstration was, I cannot help but feel that much of it was lost because of the present civil war in Nigeria and other governmental problems in Africa. There was also a very fine demonstration UNESCO library at New Delhi which established for the first time something that might approach the kind of public library service we enjoy in this country if you think in terms of the availability and free access to materials. Successful as this was, the resources which the Indian government has at its disposal do not seem to be sufficient to enable this country to repeat the same kind of demonstration in other cities.

What has UNESCO contributed to library development outside of these demonstrations in Africa and India?

Another good example would be the support given to establishing library schools in these same countries. There is one at Dakar and another in India. There was a conference in Ceylon in which we tried to point up the role that education must play in developing library service. A UNESCO representative, with excellent library experience in developing libraries, is now at work in Ceylon and in Ghana. Difficult as the problem is, I have the feeling that the forces which are being generated by UNESCO have begun to nick away at the barriers and have made some progress.

How do libraries fit into the organization of UNESCO?

There is a Division for Libraries and Archives. This division has an international advisory board and one of the members is Scott Adams, who is deputy librarian of the National Library of Medicine. So there is a direct means of communication. You know, of course, that UNESCO issues the *UNESCO Bulletin for Libraries* from its Paris headquarters.

In reading your biographical account, I recall that you received a distinguished service award. When was this and what was the award for?

Back around 1962 or 1963 I received the award from the U.S. Department of Health, Education, and Welfare. It was given primarily for my part in the administration and implementation of library legislation which had been passed. I was director of the Library Services Branch at the time. I do not know how many people are aware of it, but the library services grant legislation was one of the major breakthroughs in education; it preceded the National Defense Education Act by two years. It also preceded Sputnik, which primed the pump for the early educational grant legislation. The library grant legislation was one of the most successful undertakings of the U.S. Office of Education. One reason for this was the very close and fine cooperation which existed between the Library Services Branch and the ALA.

I have friends who think that National Library Week has served a very useful purpose and should now be allowed to die gracefully. You are in the councils of this esteemed body. What is your opinion?

I think National Library Week is very important. It was very fortunate for libraries that in 1956 we had the beginning of federal library legislation, the new public library standards, and National Library Week—all coming along at the same time. These efforts supplemented each other in a very substantial and helpful degree. National Library Week has had a great impact in bringing libraries to the consciousness of many more men and women in the street than could have been achieved in any other way. I think of this Week as making its primary contribution through the mass media—newspapers, magazines, radio, and television. I think that it is fine for local communities to have their own programs to supplement the national media exposure. Even though these do not take place in every community and in every institution, National Library Week is still valuable and important. Most laymen still do not have a real concept of what the library is able to do or even an awareness of its presence. Anything we can do to increase that awareness should be taken advantage of. The output of the National Library Week central office has been notable in terms of quality and quantity of materials. I think people who are getting tired of a National Library Week either have all the publicity they need, which I doubt, or else do not really understand the continuing need for good public relations for all types of libraries. Even aside from focusing public attention on the theme chosen for National Library Week, the organization and activities of libraries are becoming so involved and their potential importance so great that a considerable amount of energy must be devoted to explaining them to a busy public. The need for public relations for libraries, and this includes National Library Week, will grow rather than diminish.

Robert A. Miller

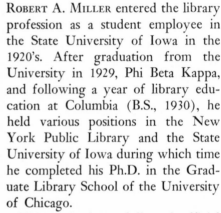

ROBERT A. MILLER entered the library profession as a student employee in the State University of Iowa in the 1920's. After graduation from the University in 1929, Phi Beta Kappa, and following a year of library education at Columbia (B.S., 1930), he held various positions in the New York Public Library and the State University of Iowa during which time he completed his Ph.D. in the Graduate Library School of the University of Chicago.

This is the bare, dull, and official account of his career up to the time of his appointment as Director of Libraries of Indiana University in 1936, but the glimpse which we have of him in Cecil Byrd's profile in the *Bulletin of Bibliography* (January-April, 1966) is anything but dull. After calling attention to his distinguished service at Indiana University in "resource development, service and management" the profile goes on to say: "To his friends and colleagues Robert A. Miller is known as a gracious host, raconteur, billiardist, and the best librarian-golfer on the circuit. As those who have worked with him can testify, he is not only an efficient and enthusiastic worker, but a kind and tolerant man of versatile talents and broad interests."

The interview was made during the visit of Dr. Miller to the University Center of Georgia, April 9, 1968, where he served as visiting scholar to the libraries of the participating institutions in the Center.

In my experience, the most difficult task of the university librarian is to assess his own position in the pattern or the web of organization and power of which he is a part. How does he find out what he can do and what he cannot do?

When you accept the position as a library administrator, you should ask the questions and get the answers which define to a large extent your responsibility to your superior and your responsibility to other people. If it is a question of authority and responsibility for branch libraries, you should seek clarification on this point. In other words you might say, "I'm not going to take this job unless there's a unified library administration." Now, I am not saying that it is important that you should have that authority, but at least it is your responsibility at the time you accept an appointment to understand what the terms are. I remember hearing such a distinguished librarian as Julian Boyd regretting that he was not a member of an administrative council where major university decisions affecting the library were being made without library representation. He felt that he should have been a member of that council. I think it may be too late after you've accepted the job to get on to such councils. I mean that proper representation can be a condition of your employment. Is there an administrative council? Is there a committee of deans? Where is the establishment of power? Do you want to be on it?

Of course, you may not be able to get into the establishment. For instance, at Indiana we are not represented on the committee on academic development, the final authority, because it is composed of the president and vice-presidents. But we're on the council of deans, the faculty council, and all library-related committees. In other words, no dean has a better committee approach to the administration than the director of libraries at Indiana. At the time of my appointment, I didn't have to ask for this representation because the groundwork had already been laid as a result of a survey sponsored by the ALA.* The president was already aware that these were necessary relationships and so he said that you will be on this and that and so on.

Do you think the majority of librarians clarify their position in the power organization of the university when appointed?

---

*Coney, Donald, and others, *Report of a Survey of the Indiana University Library*. Chicago: ALA, 1940.

I have no sympathy for the administrator who, lacking the intelligence and courage to ask for representations and to require them as a part of his employment, wonders later how he can get the job done. Later is too late. Now if you want the position as administrator so badly when you are interviewed that you lay yourself out to be agreeable, a "yes-man," then you must just take what goes with it. If you find yourself an underdog, if you find that these things are not working out the way you would like them to, it is owing to your failure to ask.

Yes, but I think you're speaking out of years of experience and perhaps don't realize that younger people seeking an administrative position may not know enough about administration to ask the right questions.

The librarian must learn. You might say to the neophyte, "If it is your desire to be an administrator, and if you have the opportunity, be sure to take enough time to understand what your position is and if it is not what you think is appropriate, then seek what you need as a condition of your employment." I think this advice would apply also when one is interviewed for lesser positions than administrative.

Do you believe that some legal authority, that is a statement of the functions of the library and of the librarian such as has often been described as the government of the library, is a useful and important thing to have in writing as a part of the official policy of the university?

I think it's a great idea, but you're not going to get it in many cases. It's the unusual university that has its charter carefully spelled out. You'll have faculty regulations, procedure manuals, personnel regulations, and such as this. But I have never been connected with a university where there was the type of code of government as proposed by Dean Wilson.* Nevertheless, if it does not exist, you can help to form it. In a conference with your superior, let's say the provost or vice-president, you might raise the question: "What do you think I should do in this particular situation?" If a decision is reached which

---

*Formerly librarian of the University of North Carolina and Dean of the Graduate Library School of the University of Chicago. See his Code of Library Government, Chapter III of *Report of a Survey of the University of Florida Library*. Chicago: ALA, 1940.

appears to establish policy, it has always been my practice on returning to my office to write it up and to send it back to the provost or vice-president. And I write something like this: "This is a summary of the conversation we had today on such and such a matter." Then I repeat the substance of our conversation, ending with a final paragraph along these lines: "If this does not correctly summarize the conversation, please let me know. If it does summarize our conversation and agreement, will you kindly initial a carbon and return it to me?"

In other words, you build up your own policy statement with respect to the government of the library by codifying decisions as they take place?

Yes.

All right now, let us turn to another question which was brought up by your reference to Dr. Boyd. Inasmuch as the university library touches every aspect of the university, especially its teaching and research, why is it that the university librarian is so infrequently represented on policy-making committees? I have the impression that few university librarians, relatively few at least, are on the really important policy-making bodies of the university. If there is a central committee to plan an institutional self-study, the librarian is not usually a member. If there is a trustee-administrative-faculty committee to plan a development program for the next ten years, the librarian may be brought into the picture but seldom appears among the decision-making group.

You referred to a survey or self-study committee. I don't think the librarian should be a member of the executive committee because he is pleading a special case. In the self-study committee in my institution, the real power was in the hands of the three men who were named to a committee. One was a political scientist, one was a scientist, and one was a professor of economics. There were no departmental chairmen or deans. I do not think the head of the library should have had a spot on the committee.

Perhaps I chose the wrong example to illustrate my question?

No. I'm speaking to this example because in our situation the report of the self-study committee was not policy until it was submitted to the faculty council, and the faculty council took action to implement certain recommendations. At this point we have policy determination and at this point the library is represented.

Do you think your own situation is typical?

I don't know. But if the guidelines you need are not a condition of employment and if you want to get clarification and help later, I think the best procedure is to work through your faculty library committee. The library committee can make representation on your behalf to the proper administrative authorities and ask that you be considered for inclusion in this or that committee or board. I am not sure that you can get into the inner power group by any sort of statutory regulation. You may get into the group because of your personal influence and reputation or standing on the campus. In other words, you may become the confidant of the president as Cameron* was at Rutgers, and obviously you must be very careful in a situation like that because presumably your advice is being asked on university rather than on library matters. It seems to me that one of the most important accomplishments of the library administrator is to establish a base of support which goes far beyond himself. The library administrator alone or as the representative of his agency is no stronger than, let's say, the purchasing agent or the head of the computing center, or any of the many other supplementary service agencies.

Now, I think you are coming close to the real solution.

The problem is how does he get the broader base? The first base must be the library committee. That is his beginning. He has a committee. And that committee should not necessarily be chosen or selected because of its interest in library matters. The members should also be chosen with reference to their value in public relations. Our universities today have a great variety of social activities. Take the cocktail circuit. It's an obvious advantage to have an articulate member of the library committee on the cocktail circuit. He can stir up debate; he can hear a lot of criticism; he can nail some criticism because he knows some of the facts. A second base is the faculty council or senate. We insert into the agenda of the faculty council about every two

*Librarian, Rutgers University, 1945-1969.

or three years a matter which the library committee could settle, but about which we prefer or pretend that we need faculty advice. When the agenda item gets into the faculty council, it comes out in mimeograph form as reported in the minutes; it is distributed to the whole faculty. At the meeting of the faculty council when this matter is under consideration, all of the chief administrators are present. Now by and large, the faculty will support the library. Some may not support it if it is a choice between departmental interests and the library, but normally if the issue is brought out in terms of specifics—we need more book money or more reference librarians—you will find all support for the library. If there is a representative of the faculty in the administrative decision-making body it is a wonderful pressure device. As a matter of fact, sometimes the pressure on my campus builds up so much on our vice-president to whom we report that when we come in he says, "Everybody is beating me over the head about the library." He doesn't mean just librarians. He means the faculty library committee, the faculty council, or even a delegation from a department.

You must have an unusually active committee. Most studies on library committees show that they are quite ineffective.

As you know, the librarian has a lot to do with the nomination of members to the committee. When it comes time to replace somebody or suggest nominations to the president, we recommend among others the names of some of our most vocal critics. We like to have critics on the library committee not only so that they can see that there's more involved in the whole matter of library operation than their particular beef, but also because they're so damned articulate. We know that wherever they go if they could begin to see our side—a risk that we run—they would become a real support to us because somebody would say, "What happened to old Wick? He used to raise hell about the library and the other day I heard him say a kind word." I realize that there may be committees where you'll not get this kind of support, but I can say honestly, and I'm sure you would agree with this, that it is up to the library administrator to get it. The library administrator can expect no program, no improvement, to come as a result of anything other than his own efforts.

What can the library committee do to bring real pressure for university library support?

Of all the committees that exist on a typical campus, the one with the most continuing prestige is the library committee. Men want to get on it if for no other reason than to be able to say, "I'm on the library committee." The chairman of the committee is a man of importance. Regardless of what college or university we're talking about, just by virtue of the fact that he is chairman of one of the most important committees of the college or university, he is in a position to call on the vice-president and say: "Joe, I've got to talk to you about the library book fund. The committee is terribly concerned about the fact that we're losing ground. Now I know you're going to receive a budget from the librarian, but I want to add my word to it independently, as a representative of the faculty library policy committee and speaking therefore for the faculty at large; I hope you can give this top attention because it is so pressing."

You mentioned a few minutes ago that one of the most distinguished librarians of recent times regretted that his library was not properly represented in the inner cabinet. If this is the case, the failure of libraries to secure representation on university policy-making boards and committees must be very high. How do you account for this?

Perhaps he never had a chance to read Wilson and Tauber's book* or enroll in a course in university library administration. When prevailed upon to take the head librarianship he had no background in the problems of administration.

Is it possible that librarians as a whole lack the administrative and intellectual ability to insure a position on such policy making boards?

I would not agree with the inference that library administrators are less influential and able than other administrators on the campus. Every new administrator has an advantage. He comes in as a new broom. He has a honeymoon period. In that period he should secure his position. After a few years there will be a new provost. There will be someone along the line who may not be a warm supporter of the library. In five or ten years the provost will move on. One must never be discouraged. When you

---

*Wilson, Louis R. and M. F. Tauber, *The University Library*. 2nd. ed. New York: Columbia University Press, 1956.

take a position you should regard it as your life work. That does not mean that you may not consider another position if you are approached later on. But I think many library administrators are career men, more interested in themselves than in the university they serve. They move from one job to another up the financial ladder. They think more of their improvement than they think of doing a sound job. The library administrator has a tremendous responsibility and a large job to do. He owes it his full loyalty and time.

Rutherford D. Rogers

WHEN Rutherford Rogers came to Yale as Director of University Libraries in September, 1969, he could look back on a career in university, public, reference, and federal libraries with great satisfaction. He had been a pioneer in undergraduate library service within the university library at Columbia University; deputy librarian of the Library of Congress and its representative at major conferences in Asia and Russia; librarian of the Rochester Public Library and founder of a county library system in which the city is located; a top administrator in several positions in the New York Public Library, and the director of libraries at Stanford. The range of his interests and the depth of his knowledge remind one of the librarians of an earlier period, such pioneering giants as Dana and Dewey; these qualities have been accompanied by a lively originality and sound business acumen. During his term of office in the New York Public Library, he contributed the idea of shelving books by size in a closed stack. In the Library of Congress he played a leading role in pioneer automation studies and in establishing the library program under Public Law 480 whereby some thirty university libraries are receiving a large portion of the publications of India, Pakistan, Indonesia, and other countries. At Stanford he proved to be an enormously successful liaison man with faculty and administrators and notably increased the role of librarians in the building of research collections.

The interview took place at Stanford University, August 13, 1968.

You have had a varied career in librarianship—public, federal, reference, and university libraries. In which type of library did you find that librarians most enjoy their work? In which do they feel most deeply involved?

Although it is hazardous to generalize, I think that the public librarian is happier and derives more satisfaction from what he is doing than librarians in most other types of libraries. The federal service is not strictly comparable. You must realize that in the federal library service a great many people are not librarians in the usual sense. They are people who work in a great institution, such as the Library of Congress, which is only primarily a library. And I think that the federal people that I know compete very strongly with the public librarian in being dedicated to their work, in their loyalty to the institution and in feeling that they are really accomplishing something. In a way this is strange because it seems to me that in a university setting you are dealing with a more cohesive clientele which has more reason to appreciate what you are trying to do for them than in any other type of library work.

Many college and university librarians do not feel that they are partners with the faculty in the educational process and are unhappy about it. Why aren't librarians more deeply involved? Is it because the two careers are basically incompatible?

You have suggested what I think is the real issue here, and that is the fact that librarians are not accepted—as perhaps they shouldn't be—as full-fledged equals of the faculty. At least on this campus they are not given faculty titles although they have academic status. But there is a great sensitivity about status among librarians here, and I am sure this is true in other universities also. There is this very strong dichotomy. In considerable part I think the blame rests with the faculty. I see it at the faculty club where the faculty has really taken control of the club as an institution. They want to make a distinction between the club as a "faculty" club and a "university" club. They are not eager to have nonfaculty people in the membership although they do admit librarians. Actually, the faculty here give more recognition to librarians as people who are participating in the educational process than to other higher salaried and higher ranking persons on the administrative staff of the university. So in part, I think, this feeling is an illusion. Nonetheless, because the library staff does not have faculty rank or title, I think this ambiguity definitely rankles with them.

Do you think this dichotomy as you express it is due perhaps to the fact that the professor is a specialist who regards librarianship as a field which requires no special knowledge but only the exercise of good judgment?

Once again, I can accept your point of view in part but I would elaborate on it. The supercilious regard of the specialist for the generalist certainly comes into play here. The specialist can speak with such authority in a very narrow field that no one can challenge him as an expert. The librarian is an expert also, but he is an expert in a much more general way. I must say that those members of the library staff who become subject specialists for one reason or another—and I speak now of the people who are curators—are highly regarded by the faculty. I think the faculty see in these librarians persons who have certain intellectual attainments which they do not see in other staff members. And to be perfectly fair to the faculty, it is true that there are many librarians who do not have any scholarly subject achievement.

Do these curators of whom you speak devote much of their time to building collections?

Yes, and in a sense our area curators know the literature of their fields much better than the faculty and therefore win the respect of the faculty because of their scholarly achievement.

I know the subject bibliographer program is an important development here and I want to return to it, but let me first ask you about another personnel matter. In the Bay area there seems to be a movement toward union membership among the librarians. Do you think the union idea is a good thing for librarians and librarianship?

I think it is very dangerous to pass a value judgment on this kind of movement. Teachers have unionized and proved that it has helped them. They have won status by virtue of having union membership. I am thinking particularly of teachers in high schools. Likewise, I think that people in the academic field are bound to look at those in the labor movement who have gained so much and to make comparisons in their situation where they have hesitated to organize and have suffered financially as a result. At Stanford we are trying to win, and are succeeding in winning, both salary and other kinds of status for librarians because we are dealing with an enlightened university administration. Our top administrators see the validity of our point of view, and we have been able to make considerable progress. A great many of the librarians have been granted sabbatical leaves; they are also eligible for other faculty benefits.

Is there not a danger that the movement toward unions may separate the librarian still further from his goal of equal status with the faculty?

If what the librarian is fighting for is status, then I find it hard to believe that he will win it by demanding it. In a university, I think you show through your academic achievement and your good work that you are worthy of being a member of important educational committees and other academic responsibilities.

One of the things younger librarians are demanding is a larger share in decision-making in the college and university library. They appear to be dissatisfied with the hierarchical channeling of all matters through department heads. Some complain that there hasn't been a general staff meeting on their campuses for twenty years. How does the librarian of a large university library find ways to take the staff into his confidence in matters of policy and administrative decision?

I think first of all that you have to create the kind of atmosphere that makes people realize that you really welcome their point of view regardless of what position they occupy on the staff. This means that you cannot merely sit in your office and issue ukases but that you actually have to go out to create a mechanism to make people realize that you are receptive to their suggestions. We have here a staff association which has been very active this past year—to a considerable extent at my invitation—in sharing with me their ideas about the kind of position struc-

The Librarian Speaking

ture and hierarchy they would like to see in the library at Stanford. I have asked them how many different grades of library positions—and this applies to the nonprofessional as well as the professional—they think there should be. Do they favor a Library Assistant I, II, III, IV type of classification or would they prefer descriptive titles such as "Supervisor of Circulation?" I not only sincerely want this advice but expect to act very largely in accordance with whatever the recommendations are simply because I think this a place where the staff has a great deal of personal interest and concern and should be listened to. The same thing is true in matters which involve more directly day-to-day operations of the library. We have created a situation where thirty to forty people on the staff participate in a very meaningful way in collection building. When you do this sort of thing it is obvious that decisions are not being made by one or two people. It is my belief that we have a much stronger organization as a result of this, and that in a multitude of counselors there is strength. It is true in book selection; it is true in a lot of other things.

You mentioned that you had asked the staff if they prefer a specific type of personnel structure and referred to such class levels as Librarian I, II, III. Do you think there is the possibility that this type of classification might present an image of civil service or clerical ranking?

I have tried to suggest to the staff that it might be desirable to move away from a hierarchical structure entirely. The basis of my argument is simply that whenever there is a series of graded steps (I, II, III, IV, etc.) no one is ever going to be happy until he is at the peak of the number of grades. On the other hand if one were simply designated a "reference librarian" who could be paid anything from an entering salary up to $12,000 a year in present times, this might be a very desirable thing. But at least on our staff, and I suspect among staffs generally, there is strong resistance to this pattern of staff classification. People want to know where they stand *vis à vis* the other people on the staff. There is a profound interest in this situation.

You have mentioned the nonprofessional staff more than once. This group presents a serious problem to university librarians because of the high rate of turnover in the staff. What

*can be done, do you think, to stabilize employment and to pro-
vide a reasonable degree of continuity in the job? It is not
entirely a matter of salary, is it?*

I am sure that low salaries have played their part in what
you have described because we have just been through this
phase, and we are beginning to come into the light on nonprofessional salaries. But I am convinced that it is more than that.
On a university campus there is a certain amount of built-in
turnover where you are employing graduate students' wives or
even faculty wives. First of all, it seems to me that older women
employees tend to be much more stable. They tend to stick
with the job, and I think we really need to direct our attention
to this market. The younger person perhaps has more opportunities pushed his or her way and is tempted to job hop whereas
I think an older person prefers the continuing job.

*Would an older person more likely expect or look to a career
position than a younger person who knows that she is only going
to remain with her present job for a year or two at the most—
the student wife, for example?*

We do not find this to be the case. On the other hand, I
think we must accept the fact that the nonprofessional staff
is by its very nature a turnover staff. I do not think that you
can avoid a substantial turnover. It has been true throughout
the thirty or more years that I have worked in libraries in
every kind of economic and geographical situation and regardless of the kind of library. Possibly in a civil service situation you
may tend to get more of the career type in a city like Rochester,
New York, where a person will start in civil service status before
marriage and continue afterward. Certainly there was a very
substantial turnover in staff at the Library of Congress, at the
New York Public Library, and there is here. Our rate of staff
turnover runs to 30 percent or more. Despite this, the library
is not as badly off in this respect as other departments on the
campus. In some departments the turnover runs as high as 39
or 40 percent.

*In other words, you feel that staff turnover in nonprofessional
positions is something libraries are going to have to live with.
In this case would it be helpful to open up some career or top
positions to nonprofessional staff members in university libraries?*

We have a Library of Congress card unit in our Catalog Division staffed primarily with nonprofessional people. We find that they do a perfectly acceptable job and turn out a tremendous amount of work in an area where it would be wasteful to use professionals. Also, we give more credit both in grade and salary to "searching" positions on the staff. We regard this as a very specialized kind of job in which the employee has to know one or several languages, not only to know them but to use them, and this we believe will help us to hold on to this type of staff member. He or she probably cannot go out into the general labor market and use these specialized skills. There is no market for them. Hopefully, we shall be able to compete for this kind of talent. I think the work is probably interesting enough so that employees will stick with it.

The turnover problem is a serious one no matter what effort is made to alleviate the condition. I feel certain that faculty and administrators generally do not realize what a terrible price we pay for this high rate of turnover. With a much larger cataloging staff this past year we did less work than the year before simply because of this lack of stability in regard to staff positions. We spent so much time training younger librarians who were not ready to do cataloging on an independent basis when they came out of library school, as well as on the training of nonprofessional people, that our production suffered. This literally cost us tens of thousands of dollars. It seems to me that the only intelligent solution to this is to try to employ experienced catalogers and to pay them enough to hold them. I think it is good business to keep catalogers who are hard to get and need a lot of special training as opposed to reference librarians who are really a drug on the market. I am impressed repeatedly with the excellent people who are available for positions in the reference field. We have a vacancy right now in general reference and have three top candidates. It is just a question of which one we prefer.

According to my figures you have done a remarkable job of raising the library's budget for books, periodicals, and binding. Your average annual growth rate in expenditures for books during the past ten years amounts to 20.9 percent, whereas fourteen of the leading privately controlled university libraries average 14.9 percent. How have you accomplished this?

We have been fortunate. Actually, in three years' time, we not only doubled the book budget but also the total library budget at Stanford. You must realize that this is not any magic on my part but partly a reflection of the situation at this University which for years had let its library dodder along and not keep pace with the rest of the University. The other units of the University took off about 1956; they built a terrifically strong faculty and student body, and it was not until 1960 that the library began to catch up. It was a slow escalation. It is true that by the time I came in 1964 the University was determined to do something about the library because of severe criticism from the faculty. In the long-range planning of the University, the library was given a high priority and it has remained so today. It stands just behind faculty salaries. And when you can get that kind of agreement and cooperation, the funds flow automatically.

Are you suggesting then that the faculty have to trigger an upsurge in library support, that without the wholehearted support of the faculty the librarian cannot hope to secure adequate funds for library support?

It is a little difficult to give you a flat answer. If I were to give one answer, however, I would say without question that faculty support is the most important factor in the picture. Choices have to be made. If the trustees, not to mention the university administration, have to be moved from a low position to a much higher position in their ranking of library need, then a certain amount of institutional compulsion is bound to creep in. They are not going to put the very substantial amounts of money that have to be put into the library in competition with other university needs unless they are convinced that it has wide spread support. I just don't think that they are going to listen to anyone but the faculty. I see signs now that the trustees of this University are beginning to wonder if they should respond to faculty requests for even further increases in library support simply because this represents such a strain on the total financial structure of the University.

In this connection, I read recently that the Association of Research Libraries has set up a committee to look into questions relating to research library management. Indirectly this may have a bearing on how the library may most effectively present

*its needs to the administration. Or it might mean that librarians
feel the need to bring in management experts to show them how
to do their job more effectively and economically. What is your
opinion about the importance of research library management
studies?*

I think a rather happy confluence of forces took place when
Dr. Fred Cole on taking office as president of the Council on
Library Resources indicated his great interest in management
studies in libraries just at a time when many of us in the field
were becoming increasingly sensitive to the desirability of this
kind of research. I was particularly sensitive coming from the
Library of Congress, because there we had an audit staff which
did much more than financial auditing. They took a very close
and critical look at the way things were done. Just before you
arrived this morning, I had some people from the controller's
office here. They were looking at our entire money-handling
and financial administrative activities. We do over a million
photocopies a year, take in a lot of money for fines, and consequently have problems connected with the receipt of income.
But they are concerned also with the way we buy our books.
We act as the purchasing agency for the University in book
buying and spend upwards of a million dollars a year. The way
we order books, the way we handle invoices, and all the mul-
tiplicity of related activities can cost a lot of money, both in
the controller's office and in our own. They are considering
the introduction of completely new techniques. For example,
Columbia University is using a technique, outside its library at
present but one which the library is considering using, whereby
the university sends to the vendor a blank check which is good
for an amount up to say $100 or $500. The vendor then writes
the check in the amount of his sales—it is a signed check—which
eliminates the necessity for him to bill the university for what
he is providing. The university makes these arrangements with
reliable, established vendors and in this way takes a lot of the
business detail off the back of the university. We are considering
such a procedure very seriously. To take another example, we
have thought it necessary to examine with great care and at
frequent intervals the status of our funds. This stems partly from
my experience at the Library of Congress where we had quarterly "status-of-funds" meetings with the fiscal staff, the Librarian of Congress, and myself. There we were dealing with

public funds which were appropriated to be spent precisely and carefully. It was a terribly serious matter if they were overspent; if they were underspent we simply lost them. So we had to administer our funds very carefully. The same was true here twenty years ago when the library book fund was less than $100,000. One spring one of my predecessors suddenly discovered that the library had overspent $15,000. Naturally there was trouble about this which produced certain controls at that time which have lived on to this day and are completely anachronistic at a time when we have generous funds and are able to spend with considerable freedom. Even if we discovered that we had overspent at the end of the year we could simply carry over invoices or borrow money from other parts of the University to tide us over until the beginning of the next year, and then proceed with a little more caution. We are not buying books just because we have ample funds. We are buying because we think they are necessary for Stanford. As I said before, we have a very broad group of people who are making decisions on a quality basis and consequently the extreme care with which we spend, guard, and watch our funds may be quite unnecessary. For this reason, I think it is a good thing to have someone who is not oriented in the same way that you are to come in occasionally and say: "Now why do you really do this? Is it necessary?" This has happened repeatedly in the course of the controller's study, and I think it is going to result in different and more economical and efficient ways of conducting our business. If this is the case, the results will benefit not only the University but also the library.

What you have spoken of is primarily a management study by your own people. Is the Association of Research Libraries concerned with local evaluation or with experts from the outside being brought in to look at management practices in general?

The Association of Research Libraries is still considering how best to structure this study, as I understand it, and a special committee has been set up to examine this matter. For example, there is the question of trying out the idea of a blank check arrangement with vendors by half a dozen research libraries at the same time, perhaps using the same group of vendors. If this technique proved to be desirable, then it is more likely to be adopted by other libraries. If I may do so without immodesty,

I would point out that what we are doing in automation, not just at Stanford but generally, is much the same sort of thing. After all, automation is a revolutionary management technique, and the fact that Columbia, Chicago, and Stanford are working together in a collaborative effort on a very broad-gauge undertaking has the same kind of management significance as other more traditional methods of research library management.

You have had experience with a new undergraduate library at Stanford. How would you advise another librarian who is planning an undergraduate library to go about the job of selecting books for the new library?

In the first place, I would hope that the librarian would think about this problem well in advance of the time of opening. If it is going to be done with care, I should recommend a planning period of a minimum of three years and desirably even longer. There is no mystery about how it is done. I am convinced that we did it the right way. We took the Lamont and Michigan lists as a base, reviewed them, did some refining ourselves, and then had about forty faculty members, spread throughout the disciplines, study and review different sections of the lists. They went through the same process of evaluation by eliminating, deleting, and adding titles. When this task was completed, we began ordering the books immediately. After three years of effort we had 40,000 volumes when we really should have had at least 60,000 for the kind of library we needed. I think we got by without great difficulty, scooted along much more smoothly when we reached 60,000 and now have approximately 75,000 volumes. We are now at the end of our second year of operation.

Not all university libraries will have the financial means to follow this procedure. They may have to rely in part on gifts, duplicates from the main library, and so forth. Do you think it is necessary to duplicate books in the undergraduate and main library?

Generally speaking, I think the undergraduate library ought to be a duplicate collection. At the beginning of my career, I worked in the Columbia College Library where we had an undergraduate library within the university library building. This simplified things in some ways because readers had access to the total resources of the university library right at hand. One might say that things are not much different here because of the proximity of the two libraries, but even so it would be less advantageous and would pose some serious problems. While I am convinced that undergraduates have needs of their own, one of the principal reasons for creating the undergraduate library was to get the undergraduate out of the way of the serious research scholar who was trying to use a complex mechanism in a very specialized way. For that reason alone, I think it is desirable to duplicate the collection. This is not as wasteful as it might seem because graduate students and faculty members who are not using books for research purposes, where they need a wide spectrum of materials, tend to go to the undergraduate library where the stacks are open and where they can quickly get the best books they need on their particular subjects. They have delightful physical surroundings. Indeed, we find that a very substantial number of persons other than undergraduates use the library.

Do you think the undergraduate library has encouraged students to choose and select books for themselves, to do more independent study and reading?

Yes. I do not have the statistics in mind but there has been an amazing increase of nonreserve materials. Because they are working in a completely open-shelf library, the students are exposed to all of these books, highly selected to be sure, but tailored pretty much to their needs and interests. We find that they are responding to this. We also performed an interesting sampling study. We found that not only are we charging out some 40 to 60 percent more nonreserve books this year than last but that last year exceeded the previous year by something like 1900 percent when there was no separate undergraduate library. We find that we are shelving many more books now which means that not only are students charging out more books for home use but they are using a great many more books within the library building.

Is there any indication that faculty have taken advantage of new facilities to encourage less dependence upon the textbook and library reserve reading?

Well, you must realize that at Stanford there is a great deal of what I suppose one might call progressive teaching where the instructor doesn't just rely on the reserve book collection. There are many undergraduate honors courses and undergraduate seminars where students do the kind of independent reading which I think you are talking about. One of my great concerns about this library, which cost the University over $5 million, was that we might just have a kind of grandiose reserve book reading room, a great study hall of reserve books. I want to have as the head of this library a librarian who will work with the faculty to try to insure that we are making the maximum use of all the potentials of the facility. We could, of course, operate the library efficiently under good technical direction, but I have chosen the latter course. I might mention also that the undergraduate library has an elaborate audiovisual set-up. We have had good response from this, although I do not believe we have yet begun to reach its full potential.

Someone has said that without some sort of library guidance a college or university library is like a great power plant with the transmission lines down. Do you feel the need for any kind of instruction in the use of the library on this campus?

We not only feel the need but for years we have offered a course to undergraduates. For the first time last year we started a "team instruction" experiment with five reference librarians in the undergraduate library participating. Although we have not had a large student response, the thing we feel the need for is once again to be able to teach this course in collaboration with either the "Western Civilization" or the basic English courses in the University. This is where I think we have lost ground, something I want a new librarian to try to re-establish. In this same connection, I might mention that we are employing a new curator for Latin American materials. The faculty of the Hispanic program has set up a course which they want him to teach. It is encouraging when the faculty see the need and invite the library expert in the field to come in to teach the course.

If I understood you correctly, you feel that your under- graduate course in library instruction would be more successful if it were taught in connection with one of the student's regular courses.

Yes, and may I say that we do this with graduate students.

For example, we invite the history and political science professors to bring their students into the library to go through our documents division, to learn about the special indexes, to see the collections we have, and to find out how to use them under the guidance of our four specialists in state, federal, foreign, and international documents. We find that this type of instruction pays off. The circulation of our document division has doubled in three years. Now this is a result of getting out and doing a job with the faculty. We do this in other ways. We invite the English faculty to bring their graduate students in for a general tour of the library. A year ago I conducted a group through myself and showed them how to use some of our microtexts which they would not have known about otherwise. I showed them how to use the indexes and where things were in the reference room and in the stacks.

You have a service to business and industry known as the Technical Information Service. How did this service come into being?

TIS was born as a device to protect Stanford and its interests from indiscriminate use of our materials by outsiders. By this I do not mean that the University gives any less service. As a matter of fact, now that we have TIS, I think that we probably give more service to industry on the Peninsula, but we do it under controlled conditions. First of all, we produce a great deal more photocopy instead of losing control of the book itself. Where books are loaned, there is a staff which can get them back in, say, twenty-four hours. It is really a highly organized service. The University doesn't make money on it. If you take into account the wear and tear on the collection and the fact that you have created a great research library which is usable by industry, we are not really being paid for it. We get our direct service costs back and that is all. That is all we expect. After all, most of this industry grew out of Stanford. We have local multi-millionaires who were once Stanford students and professors. Using ideas on which they worked at Stanford, they have established their own businesses, sometimes in garages. From very small beginnings, some have grown to several thousand employees with a hundred-million-dollar-a-year production. As a University we receive support from industry; so I think this service is not only a good thing for industry but it is also a good thing for Stanford.

Do you see in this "service to industry" extension of university library service an opportunity for substantial federal support?

I doubt if there will ever be substantial federal support. The State Technical Services Act might provide some support for this but I doubt if it would be any more lucrative than what we receive from business itself. It would merely shift support from industry to government.

Under your direction Stanford has gone a long way in the direction of having its librarians assume the major responsibility for selection and building collections. Is it necessary to have full-time specialists for this purpose?

In a library doing the magnitude of collecting in which we are engaged, there is no question about it. This is very much a full-time job, heavily supported by bibliographical assistants. Also you should realize that these people have certain demands placed on them for reader-service because of their specialized knowledge. When the faculty realize that there is someone in the library who knows more about the collections in their particular fields than they do, they not only come to him for assistance but refer their graduate students to him. In an ideal set-up, I think it is desirable to have the subject specialists located near the reference department where they can function in a dual capacity as builders of collections and guides to the library's resources.

Is it very difficult to find people who combine librarianship with an advanced degree in a subject field for this kind of work?

Yes, it is difficult, and I would say that one of the least important qualifications is formal library education. The indispensable thing is a thorough knowledge of the subject field in which they are performing their curatorial duties. For example, we try to get people with the doctorate in Germanics, Romance languages, Slavic, and the Latin-American fields. We believe that we have been successful for the most part in recruiting such candidates.

Judging from the qualifications you require of your biblio-graphers, you are competing for persons trained for college teaching. Are they likely to make the switch or to stay put?

In some cases they are happy to remain, but you must be very careful in your selection. We have batted some foul balls here. We imported one man from Germany who, it turned out later, really wanted to teach. Unfortunately, we paid his expenses to move. After he had worked in the library for about six weeks, he informed me that he was going to accept a teaching position in another college in the state the following September. At the time of recruitment, you must have a clear understanding with the candidate that the bibliographer's job is not a stepping-stone to teaching. As a matter of fact, I think it is a great mistake to employ anyone in this capacity who is going to share his time between teaching in the classroom and working in the library. In no time at all, you are going to lose this man to teaching.

Walter A. Sedelow, Jr.

WALTER SEDELOW, JR., is a master of pace who literally streaks across the fields of history, sociology, and computer science. Born in 1928, educated at Amherst (B.A., 1947) and Harvard (M.A., 1951; Ph.D., 1957), he has had a fabulously varied career in a very short span of time: Captain U.S.A.F. Reserve, instructor at Williams College and Amherst, and associate professor of history and sociology at Parsons and Rockford, where he served also as chairman of the departments in both colleges.

Dr. Sedelow doesn't try to be different from most librarians; he is. Basically, he is an historian with a scientist's inquiring mind. He has added a provocative new dimension to the deanship of the School of Library Science at North Carolina, to which he was appointed in 1967 after serving Chapel Hill in a joint appointment in the Department of Sociology and the Department of Information Science.

The interview took place on November 1, 1968, at the Americana Hotel, Miami Beach, Florida.

When Archibald MacLeish became Librarian of Congress, many librarians wondered why on earth he did it. Some asked why a poet would take a job which left him little time for writing; others asked why he took a job for which "he was so patently unfitted." Although you are not a poet, you are an historian and I should like to pass this same question on to you.

Your reference to Archibald MacLeish is an interesting one in a trivial way because his mother was prominently associated with one of those many colleges which claim precedence among women's colleges, Rockford College, where Jane Addams was in the first graduating class; Archibald MacLeish returned to Rockford and I heard him talk there. I can still remember from my undergraduate days hearing people at Amherst discuss the great stir when he was chosen Librarian of Congress. I recently turned up in the archives of the library school at Chapel Hill a telegram of protest which was sent off to Washington to complain about this "most unsuitable appointment."

I am not totally without prior association with libraries. As Ralph Ellsworth said to me once, everybody in the academic world has a certain kind of competence as to libraries just because they tend to be users of them. But beyond that, I had the good fortune to attend Melvil Dewey's college, where he was still something of a hero; and as an undergraduate I did some work in the Amherst College Library, now the Robert Frost Library. One summer when a member of the professional staff was unable to get to Amherst as soon as originally expected, I filled in as a sort of full-time library employee. That, of course, is pretty small stuff.

As you probably know, I am a professor of computer and information science at Chapel Hill, as well as of sociology, and I suppose that one of the relevancies for the development of my association with the Chapel Hill library school is this involvement with the utilization of computers and other kinds of technology which are just around the corner and which, more than likely, are going to have dramatic effects on libraries and information systems.

There are other considerations, too, which I might mention. As with so many other social institutions and organizations, great changes are coming to libraries and information systems. This would seem to me to imply far more effective application not only of operations research techniques and the like, but also of social behavioral science research techniques, in order to evaluate the effectiveness of different methods of handling information. So it is not only my computer and information science background that has relevance, perhaps, but also the expectation

that the role of the social sciences in the world of library science—
and, of course, I count myself a sociologist—is going to be an
increasingly significant one.

To put the matter in a rather different set of terms, I was
asked by the chancellor to serve on the committee for the
selection of a dean for the library school, and while I was off in
California on a trip, the rest of the committee met and suggested
that the University might perhaps try to interest me in this
position.

*It has been frequently charged in the past that librarians have
sinned by courting the technician and neglecting scholarship.
Will the present flight toward more and more technology sub-
merge still further the librarian's scholarly interests and understanding?*

I would like to think it is not a matter of either technological
and scientific competence *or* greater scholarly depth that we
are seeking, but rather both. There has been a certain amount
of what students sometimes call "mickey-mouse" activity in
library schools. Giving a student graduate school credit for
neatness in typing cards is not my idea of an appropriate
sort of academic activity and does lay the university open to the
charge that some of its critics, particularly some on the European
side, have leveled, on occasion, at American institutions. So with
a restructuring of graduate school curricula in library science
there may very well come a day when we shall have both a
greater maturity on the technological and scientific side of library education and also a greater scholarly depth. I think that
the kinds of technological concerns that are going to come to
the fore in library science in the years ahead will be radically
different from those of the past. That may raise a question as
to the desirability of attempting to transpose the attitudes of
some academics toward certain of the things that librarians have
been doing to a new set of attitudes toward people who will
be involved on the technological side of libraries of the future.
For instance, with all due regard to the importance of looking
into questions concerning card-file drawers and the like, that
range of technical concern is not what the technology of the
future has in store for the librarian. I think, too, that as the
problems of providing knowledge for Americans loom ever
more centrally in our minds, we will allocate more rewards to

try to get good strong minds involved in information systems work. As the reward structure improves, there will be a heightened status for librarians if the experience we have had with status phenomena in other fields holds, as I expect it will. Now at the same time that all this is taking place, and without wanting to get into the battle over the role of library technicians, I think that we are going to see a great deal of occupational stratification within the library world. Many sorts of routine activities will be assigned to a different type of person than the well-trained librarian of the future. You can take the analogy of a physician, for instance, and the kinds of things which are now done for him by helpers of one sort or another, such as nurses, medical technicians, and the like. I think that when we have more thoroughly trained librarians—well educated in cultural depth as well as in the understanding of the relevance of science to the design of systems which are appropriate to library and information systems work—there will be less reluctance to let some of these other roles be assigned to people who have another kind of education.

In many university libraries of the West Coast, possibly elsewhere, librarians are assuming a much greater responsibility for book selection than they have in the past. This is one place where we need librarian-specialists. You implied that there are other opportunities for librarians of specialized training of the type you are speaking about. Would you care to elaborate?

First, I would like to make one point in a prefatory way. Originally I was an historian. While I am not opposed to being thought of in terms of computer science and the like, I also see myself in the tradition of the historian-librarian. You know, for example, that there have been at least three prominent historians in the past century who have served as librarians of Harvard, of whom John Fiske was the first. So I do not want to seem like either one or the other kind of specialist at the very time when I am making the point that I don't think there has to be a choice between science and technology on the one hand and cultural depth on the other.

To come to the point with reference to your question as to how much demand there may be for persons of cultural and scientific depth as librarians, I think it is certainly true in collection building that there is a trend in many universities for the selection process to be ever more in the hands of the professional librarian—a trend with which I think there are perhaps advantages in not moving too rapidly—which, of course, does make for important and increasing roles for library scientists in the selection process. But I think that is only a part of the reason we need to have greater subject matter depth—say on the scale of competence which the University of Michigan has sought for among its library science doctoral students, where they require the equivalent of a master's degree in a subject field. And that larger demand is a function of greatly enhanced demand levels that I see emerging for highly qualified reference assistance. I see the subtlety and depth, as well as the number of questions reference people are going to have to answer, as increasing markedly. As our society becomes more knowledge-dependent, and as changes take place in perhaps the model personality structures of Americans, we are going to find that reference questions are being asked even by some youngsters who haven't gotten through the twelfth grade which not so many decades ago we would have thought were rather good questions for upperclassmen in colleges to ask. So I think that as part of what I see as a growing centrality of the accessibility of knowledge of all sorts to an ever increasingly large cut of the total society, the demand for librarians who are knowing as to the substance of knowledge itself will dramatically increase.

Some sociologists—Talcott Parsons[*] would be one of them— feel that among American institutions, like the family, the church, and so on, education is at least on the verge, and maybe over the verge, of becoming the central institution of our society. I think that is certainly a point of view which can be effectively defended. Within our lifetimes I rather imagine the immensely enhanced importance of education that we see the beginnings of now will be with us indeed, and in that world it may even be that people will feel that they have a right to knowledge. I think, too, that we may be moving toward a situation in which the classroom as the model of the learning situation is on the verge of becoming passé. I suspect that more and more the characteristic learning situation is going to be the laboratory, the studio, and the direct access to the information transfer function achieved through technology. And it may just be that

---

[*]Professor of Sociology, Harvard.

some of the functions which are now fulfilled in the classroom will be far more adequately coped with through the mobilization of science and technology to make information accessible to the student regardless of where he is. In that situation the role of the librarians of the future could be dramatically enhanced.

Will the kind of information service which you are fore-casting remain under the umbrella of librarianship or will it become so highly specialized that it will be decentralized as the function or functions of a number of different agencies?

A lot depends on what happens to the quality of education for librarians—not only their graduate education, but the kinds of pre-graduate school educational experiences of those who decide to go into librarianship. Hopefully, we shall get ever stronger students in library science, as a function in part of seeing there are more opportunities, both financial and intellectual, in the library world than ever before. I think it is also true that much depends on the substantive content of library and library-related higher education. If it drags its heels too badly, librarians will find themselves bypassed, and instead of having important roles in the management of library and information systems, they will be superseded by people who more thoroughly understand the kinds of systems that are going to be developed. Already on various campuses I can see a tension developing between library administrators and people who are involved in the provision of management information systems for colleges and universities, as to who is going to have the administrative oversight for the people who provide the systems support for libraries. Now many of the resolutions to those tensions on individual campuses in which the librarian has, at least for the time being, won out, are potentially very unstable resolutions, unless those librarians (and, more likely, their successors) are able to acquire more competence than they currently have to enable them to oversee effectively this new technology.

As I said earlier, there will be a great deal of structural differentiation and specialization within the broad field of library and information science, so that just as we have people with special knowledge and general knowledge now, we'll have even more of such variety in years to come. There will be a great deal more specialization at the same time that there will be a change in the understanding of what's involved in systematically meeting the knowledge and information needs of individuals, organizations, institutions, and political entities, so that we will have a new core of what might be called library and information systems education.

Do you see evidence of the type of person you need to build this new library structure coming into the library schools now?

Yes, I think that I see some; there has been some movement in this direction already. I think, for example, of two students whom I taught at Amherst, one of whom is an assistant to Richard De Gennaro, the associate librarian at Harvard for systems. This young man was originally a chemistry major. We have just had the pleasure of adding to the library school faculty at Chapel Hill a young man who had been an honors student in mathematics at Amherst, who is now completing his work for the doctorate in library science. They are signs of a changing world. It is also true that on the information science side, we attract some very bright people indeed. Many of them are going to find their way in one fashion or another into roles which have a vast import for library work. In our society, the provision of material reward makes a great deal of difference as to who goes after what jobs. As the demands for certain sorts of skills becomes ever more apparent—skills which are relevant to the meeting of knowledge needs of various kinds—the salaries and other rewards will go up and that in turn will lead to a shift in the kinds of people whom we get in library schools. That is not to say that there have not been many good people in library schools for a long time. Particularly with so many other professions shut off to women, librarianship has been the beneficiary of many enormously talented people who might have gone elsewhere. So I do not want to minimize the quality of student and professional persons in the library field. But I think we should be getting not only more of them but also attracting some new types of people who, modally, are probably somewhat more aggressive, more intellectual, and, especially, scientifically inclined. At the same time, as I have said, there will be this differentiation of role in the field so that certain jobs which are now assigned to newly-graduated library school persons will be assigned to other people.

The University of Chicago has begun to operate, in recent years at least, along some of the lines you are suggesting for the future. Is there any noticeable difference so far as you know in the type of library school student they are attracting and graduating from those who attend the more traditional type of school?

It is rather too soon to say. Dean Don R. Swanson has not been at Chicago all that long. Incidentally, I think a pervasive influence there could be that of Victor H. Yngve, who came from M.I.T., perhaps principally to the Chicago library school but also to the Committee on Information Science. He is founder of the *Journal of Machine Translation* and a former colleague of Noam Chomsky, professor of linquistics at M.I.T. Yngve has now been drafted to chair the entire graduate program in Computer and Information Science at Chicago, so the extent to which he will be able to concentrate on matters in the library school is a question. William Cooper is another "new style" professor there, who—if memory serves—took his doctor's degree at Berkeley in the logic and method of science; these three men cannot help but have an impact on the library school. I have met some of the graduate students at Chicago and it is my impression that there is some change, although I speak from ignorance on the immediate past during Dean Asheim's* day. However, I do see the contrast clearly between some of these young people who have come under the influence of Yngve, Swanson, and others and those of the "classic generation" of the Chicago school during L. R. Wilson's day.

One of the areas in which librarianship is being transformed more rapidly than in others has to do with the health sciences. In that situation it is not surprising that one of the ways in which librarianship is being altered—and this applies to Chicago— is through the training of people for medical librarianship. I think that we shall see that Swanson's influence is particularly notable through the first generation of his students in that area.

Substantial changes are now under way at Carolina which we hope will make of Carolina both a traditional school and a very modern one. This year we have the good fortune to have on our faculty one of the most proficient young mathematicians to be associated with any library school in the country. Dr. Gary Koch, who has published in *Technometrics, Biometrics,* and

---

*Lester E. Asheim, Dean, Graduate Library School, University of Chicago, 1952-1961.

Mathematical Bioscience, and who has done a dissertation in statistics as applied to information retrieval, is giving a course in library administration that is to familiarize students with the methods of quantitative measurement which are commonly associated with operations research and which have potential for the analysis and evaluation of library systems. Not only that, but we are in the process of cross-listing for library science three courses in the machine-aided analysis of language, such as you would use in conjunction with information retrieval, automatic abstracting, and the like; and we will next move to the possibility of cross-listing courses on the systems side. While not losing power on the cultural side, I think that we shall very quickly find ourselves in a class with UCLA and the new school at SUNY Buffalo as to quantitative capability.

Let me turn to some specific questions in the field of library automation, questions facing many library administrators today. Number one: is there a certain point in the volume of library circulation, annual or daily circulation, beyond which automated circulation control is recommended or is more practical than manual methods from a financial point of view?

That is a multi-variant situation, so to speak. You can't make decisions wisely on the basis of the one dimension you mention. This is one of the reasons why, beginning this year, we are introducing to our library school students techniques of applied mathematics and operations research of the sort that are needed if we are going to develop the models for making decisions on matters of the kind you mention. You have to take into account a number of different variables, and look at the different pay-off implications and the different cost implications. I do not think there is a simple answer and probably it would be misleading to produce any.

Well, here is a related question where there is perhaps more experience on which to base an answer. Circulation is sometimes heralded as the logical place to make a beginning in automation. Should automated circulation control be undertaken if finances do not allow the creation of book cards for all books in the collection at the time of change?

I would be remiss in my duty if I were to give an off-the-cuff answer to your question. If I were in Atlanta I would be inclined to talk at length with John Hamblen* at the Southern Regional Education Board; he was one of the pioneers in getting a circulation control system set up—at Southern Illinois University at Carbondale. Generally speaking, we tend to underestimate the short-term costs of these undertakings. They turn out to be more expensive than is often supposed, at the same time that we are even more underestimating as to their long-term utility. One factor that we are all aware of, and will be increasingly aware of in the future in making these decisions, is the evolution of networks with various sorts of standardization, which will make new developments possible in libraries. It may be that for decisions which an institution might delay at a given moment for itself it will be inclined to move on a little sooner insofar as possibilities for network operation become real— where the utilization of a computer is part and parcel of this business of standardization.

Does the use of MARC tapes in their present stage of development have significant advantages in the production of catalog cards over the use of xeroxing title II-C cards?

I think one should get an opinion there from a person who is more deeply involved. I did attend the sessions at Kansas City on the state of the MARC project** and I have read some of the literature, but I know there are many others far better informed than I am. Taking the long view, I will say that in the next five to ten years there is no question in my mind that the MARC project is worthy of very considerable support, not only financial support within the government but cooperation from within the academic community. Now I do think that it is too bad that the format established wasn't of sufficient generality to accommodate a larger subset of the total potential titles that could be included. I think there are some stresses here as to the prospective utility of the MARC project in the short run which wouldn't be there if they had made certain other decisions on formating.

Is the use of a small computer for many library operations, the computer housed in the library, recommended as opposed

---

*Special Project Director, Computer Sciences, S.R.E.B.

**The Machine Readable Cataloging project, MARC, was conceived as an experiment to test the feasibility of producing and distributing machine readable cataloging data.

to use by the library of a large centrally-located university computer?

Again, there isn't one good answer. I might say that I think the question wouldn't be formed in that way if the awareness of what is involved in computers were greater than it is. The practical meaning of that statement is a plea for being sure that library education in the future includes the kind of exposure which would enable another generation to formulate questions which are more satisfactory. Again, the question of the large computer versus the small is one in which I should say there is not a clear answer, for many applications purposes, even within the community of computer specialists, as distinct from library specialists. It is unclear at the moment just what direction the technology of the computer is going to take. I think we are going to get not only far bigger and more powerful computers, but that we are also going to get ever smaller, and (relative to their scale) more powerful computers. Again, a decision as to which to use is not a simple one. If it is going to be rightly made it implies the use of kinds of operations and systems analysis approaches that I take it down in your state of Georgia Dr. Slamecka* is trying to train people to be able to handle. There are those in the computer field who were all for big computer installations and they view small computers in many different settings as balkanization so to speak; and there are other people who live in balkan states and like it that way. We can see both kinds of solutions on different campuses.

There is another question, too, which you may not want to get into here, but it has to do with some of the roles computers are going to have in handling vast bodies of information: to what extent its power as a switching device will be employed, rather than what has preoccupied us, at least at the level of general thought and to some extent of application, the computer as a storage device. The question is, do you try to put the content of the Library of Congress into the machine as in an earlier day was proposed; or do you use other developments in technology which make for micro-micro miniaturization, so to speak, and then use the computer as the device for picking out from sets of materials which may, in noncomputer form, be present

*Vladimir Slamecka, Director, School of Information Science, Georgia Institute of Technology.

in lots of sites, and with the computer direct the extraction of the relevant parts and control the reprographic provision to the user of what he wants? There are possibilities on that side which were not at all as clear five years ago as they are now. This is a good time to emphasize that the prospective impact on libraries, information systems, and library science of technology is far from being exhausted by a concern for the computer. That is only one, and in its present form only one part of one, of the kinds of technology that are going to make an extraordinarily vast difference to us in the years ahead.

James A. Servies

LIBRARIANS who have the good fortune to be free in the planning of library services to make a clean start with no hobbles of pre-existing patterns may be the envy of their colleagues in the academic library field. But it must not be forgotten that they are sometimes faced with the difficult task of building a university library collection without benefit of faculty advice and clearly formulated objectives to help assess the trends and to provide adequately for tomorrow's tomorrow. Such was the case at the University of West Florida.

In this interview which took place in May, 1968, on the newly-created campus at Pensacola, James Servies describes some of the problems which he encountered in building a collection from scratch. Mr. Servies was born in 1925, studied at the University of Chicago (Ph.B., 1947; M.A. L.S., 1949), and served an apprenticeship in librarianship in the circulation and reference departments of the universities of Chicago, Miami, and the College of William and Mary. Before becoming librarian of William and Mary in 1957, he compiled his first publication, *A Bibliography of John Marshall* (1956); a second bibliography, *Earl Gregg Swem, a Bibliography* in 1960; and edited *The Poems of Charles Hansford* (1961) in collaboration with C. R. Dolmetsch. He came to his present position as director of libraries of the University of West Florida in 1966.

As a librarian who has had the opportunity as well as the obligation to build a college library collection overnight, what steps did you follow to select and develop this collection; and what changes, if any, in procedure would you follow if you had the chance to do it all over again?

Well, let's take the first question. The first problem a librarian faces in developing a college or university library collection overnight, so to speak, has nothing much to do with the selection of individual books. When you start from scratch, as we did in an office on the fifth floor of a suburban shopping center, the first order of business is to get on the mailing lists of publishers and bookdealers. Bear in mind that you have a desk that is perfectly empty, very few staff members, and perhaps only a secretary. The question is what to do first. I discovered that I was continually turning around for a directory or a book-trade bibliography and we didn't have any. So one of the first things we did was to place a blanket order with Bowker, and then we spent two or three weeks writing nothing but postcards asking dealers, agents, jobbers, publishers, and others to place us on their mailing lists.

The second problem was to develop a basic collection. Our development phase took place before the publication of the California list,* but there were other comprehensive lists available. We were working in January, February, March, or thereabouts, of 1966. After talking with friends in Virginia, Delaware, and elsewhere, I decided that the soundest way to go about building a collection would be to use as a basis the undergraduate library assembled at the University of Michigan. I bought its shelf list on microfilm, sent in to New Orleans where a Xerox Copyflow facility was available, and had the copy trimmed to 3″ x 5″ size, alphabetized, and searched in the "in print" sources. We were then ready to order. This gave us a pretty sound, basic undergraduate collection, at least of "in stock" or "in print" materials.

How much time did you have to acquire and prepare for the shelves the initial collection before classes were formerly in

---

*Books for College Libraries: A selected list of approximately 53,400 titles based on the initial selection made for the University of California's New Campuses Program. . . . Chicago: ALA, 1967.

session and approximately how much money was involved in acquiring the foundation collection?

I came on board in April, 1966. The first class of junior-level students was admitted to the University in September, 1967. So we had about seventeen months. I hope other new institutions will be lucky enough to have even more time, although we certainly had a better start than most.

Our president fought for and obtained a budget sufficient to acquire a basic collection of 100,000 volumes. A per-volume cost of $8.00 was also justified, thus resulting in a development budget, spread over one biennium, of $800,000.

In selecting your foundation collection, I am sure that you did not aim at any fixed number of titles. Perhaps the ultimate size was largely determined by the amount of money you had. But still you must have had some measuring stick as to the number of titles that could be purchased in each subject if only to bar out those enthusiasts (or your own enthusiasm) from spending all the money on particular subjects. How did you manage a reasonable distribution among subjects?

Unfortunately, we didn't; perhaps just as well, for we had no faculty and the structure of the curriculum was still under discussion. However, I recall the distribution of subjects worried me then, and I found that occasional review of the rapidly-growing shelf-list was necessary to guide our acquisitions.

I think you said that your first choices were made on in-print titles?

Precisely. There were some problems in variations of edition which we cleared up as we went along. We found, of course, that the Michigan list was more than an in-print selection. I had met one of the men who participated in the assembly of the collection, and he told me of some of its peculiarities; that is, that the undergraduate library was a result both of a selection of in-print materials and of specific titles requested by the faculty. Obviously, the faculty choices included a high percentage of out-of-print material as well as a very good selection of foreign titles which we are "blocking up" and hope to buy when funds permit. The Michigan list, then, was our principal guide in making our initial selections. There is an interesting correlation between the California and the Michigan lists—many major works appear in both. Since the undergraduate library of the University of Michigan was formed in 1962, we made use also of its supplementary shelf list which covered the period, 1962-1965. Therefore, when we started, we were only about a year or two out-of-date. For coverage from 1965 on, we used fairly comprehensively the entries cited in *Choice*.

Who selected the books from Choice?

I selected them myself. We had very little staff at that time.

Was there no faculty?

We had no faculty. We pulled titles from the subject categories according to our best judgment at that time of the future curriculum offerings of the University. Another plan we followed was to acquire complete collections. It had always been a stated objective of the University that a full program in marine biology be established. At the outset, we acquired a collection of current materials in marine biology at a cost of several thousand dollars from a dealer in Washington, D. C. We also bought a collection of recent monographs displayed at a meeting of the National Council of Teachers of English. A large collection in the fields of psychology and educational psychology was obtained from the estate of a former dean at a Mid-West institution. We bought another collection of materials in the field of education from a library in New York which was going out of business. All of these collections, of course, excluded periodicals. We began with purchases of monographic material only. We also bought, on my own selection, a large number of sets from Barfield. The selection of reference material was made initially on the basis of the Enoch Pratt Free Library's brief guide to *Reference Books*. Since this provided only a basic selection, we added to it from Winchell.

In the past we have stressed the importance of building collections to fit a particular institution's needs. We have talked with pride of regional and local differences. But in basing our selections largely on standard lists such as the Michigan and California lists, and adding to them from the selections in Choice, *aren't we really saying that all basic collections should be alike, that what is good for Guilford, N. C., is also good for Pensacola, Florida?*

I rather hope we can say this. A basic collection, by definition, is based on some consensus of excellence in library holdings for a certain level of academic offerings. Of course, I do not imply that total holdings should be the same everywhere. Certainly regional, human, and accidental factors will soon enable each collection to develop its own personality.

You found the Michigan list most helpful in making your initial selection. This is basically an undergraduate listing. Did you know at the outset that you had to build for graduate work in certain fields? If so, how did this affect selection? For example, in a beginning undergraduate collection, I suppose one could largely ignore foreign language material except in a limited number of fields?

We knew the University would expand rapidly into graduate work. Several disciplines, clearly, were to be among the first to be involved. Therefore, we had some evidence with which to justify acquisitions over and above our basic holdings. Foreign language materials are essential here, but by and large the major cost factor in supporting graduate studies is involved in the back files of periodicals and serials.

You mentioned earlier the difficulty of starting from scratch with practically no staff and without the book-trade tools which we normally take for granted in ordering books. Did you give any thought to making use of a commercial firm, once you had made your selections, for ordering and cataloging your material?

Yes, we considered several commercial firms, one of them quite seriously. Upon careful study, however, we decided we could do the job better. Besides, the State of Florida had appropriated funds for books—not for books and processing. We had a good staff, although of quite limited numbers, and they were able to use the budget in the most efficient way.

When you got around to periodicals, what did you use as a guide in selection?

The development of journal files was one of our most important tasks. In view of the fantastic rise in the price of both original hard copy and reprints—the cost of microtext had been a little more stable—it seemed obvious that we would be spending a fairly high proportion of our funds on journals. We had to decide whether to buy in the original, reprints, or micro-text, how comprehensive we should be in total coverage, and how far back we should go in acquiring back files of individual titles. Decisions were made—in some cases right, in other cases wrong.

Did you find such a standard list as Farber's Classified List of Periodicals for the College Library *of any help in selection?*

No, this was too out-of-date. We used the list of periodicals on current subscription at William and Mary, a fine list which had just been revised before I came to Florida. Additions and dele-tions to this list were made on the basis of our curriculum struc-ture and the appearance of titles in one or more of the primary indexes.

Was your selection of titles influenced by what was indexed in the general Wilson periodical indexes?

These titles were given a very high priority.

How far back did you find it necessary to begin your files of individual titles?

There is some published research which is helpful here. But in general we purchased comprehensive runs in those areas in which we had reason to believe the University would build great strength. In the sciences we established a more arbitrary date. For the most part we purchased files from 1950 on. In the humanities, as well as in some scientific subjects, such as mathematics, we felt the need for more complete files. We varied the depth of the file, therefore, according to the nature of the title itself. I spent a weekend in New York talking to one agent about our list of approximately 1,000 serial titles which we decided to acquire in an initial purchase. With his help, I went through the list to see in what form we should try to buy the sets—whether, for example, a title such as Liebig's *Annalen* was available in the original, reprint, or microtext and at what cost. Much of the selection, frankly, was affected by the availability of titles and the financial realities of the back-file market.

Since you acquired quite a few back files in microtext form, what has been your experience regarding reader use of this

*material? Has it been used? Do you believe the form of the
material has hindered use in any way?*

It has been used, but certainly not as much as hard copies.
Most of the readers on the market today are poor, and some
are terrible. Practically every type of user, from the most in-
nocent freshman to the sophisticated Ph.D., has some difficulty
with technique. Also, as you know, print-out capability varies
according to the media involved. Consequently, most users will
avoid microcards unless they are in the final state of desperation.

*You mentioned that your initial choices were limited to in-
print material. What procedures did you follow in selecting and
acquiring out-of-print materials?*

When dealers' catalogs began coming in, we worked quickly
on marking and ordering large numbers of titles in our major
fields. The size and scope of our projected collection was such
that we could take short-cuts. A smaller library, with fewer
funds, would have had to develop a desiderata list, then begin
looking around for the outlets that would have those titles in
stock. Since we needed so much, we could purchase according
to lists of available material. Of course, I bought extensively at
various stores throughout the United States, when I felt the
prices were good. I probably bought at least 10,000 volumes
just in the smaller o.p. stores in Florida, and was able to reduce
substantially the per volume cost of acquisition. It is easy, with
fairly large amounts of money, to send bulk orders to publishers.
But it is also one of the most expensive ways of acquiring a basic
stock. Another savings, I think, resulted in our buying quite a
few titles from the Michigan list through the second-hand "textbook" market. This most profitable technique, administered
through our bookstore, resulted only in a few returns and
brought in basic titles at a greatly reduced overall cost.

*I think I have a fairly clear picture of what you actually did
in building your initial collection. Now tell me what you would
have done differently if you were starting afresh.*

One thing I would do would be to take immediate steps
to acquire files of all the major journals we might need for at
least the past fifteen years, say from 1950 on, instead of concentrating, as we did, on long runs of back files of certain
journals. One of the problems every library runs into in its

development stage is the indefinable nature of the curriculum of its college or university. This takes time. To the degree to which objectives of the institution can be made clear at the outset, to that extent the librarian's task is greatly simplified and made manageable. If there is "blue-skying," if there is indecision about the subjects to be taught, or if there is uncertainty regarding objectives, the librarian's chances of error are multiplied. To take one example, in 1966 we were buying with the understanding that the University would offer geology courses. In 1968, we had no geology department. I now have a certain number of dollars tied up in geology journals which might better have been spent on education, business, or history. I would stress that the librarian needs first to seek the greatest degree of intelligence with regard to where the university is going.

One other thing, I regret that we did not acquire more of the titles indexed in the *Reader's Guide*, the *Social Science Index*, and other general periodical indexes.

Eldred R. Smith

ELDRED SMITH is one of the leading young librarians on the West Coast. As his name has appeared more and more frequently in connection with championing the rights and privileges of professional librarians ("Librarians and Unions: The Berkeley Experience," *Library Journal*, 93:717-20, February 15, 1968), he has become something of a controversial figure among California librarians and administrators. He is presently serving as president of the Librarians' Association of the University of California, established January, 1968, which includes more than five hundred librarians employed by the University.

The interview took place on the Berkeley campus in the summer of 1968 where Mr. Smith serves as Head of the Search Division of the University of California, Berkeley, Library. He received his B.A. and M.A. (English) from the University of California, Berkeley, in 1956 and 1962, and the M.S.L.S. degree from the School of Librarianship of the University of Southern California in 1957. In 1969 he was awarded a Council on Library Resources fellowship to study the role of specialization in university librarianship.

I think you told me you were president of the Librarians' Association of the University of California. What is this organization? What are you trying to do?

It includes all librarians employed by the University, and it was established to provide a recognized academic voice for the University of California librarians in the affairs of their own University, something similar to what the faculty has in the academic senate.

Is membership automatic if one is a librarian?

Everyone is automatically a member if he is working half-time or more for the University and is classified as a librarian. Some professionally trained librarians, who are not classified as librarians, are unfortunately excluded the way things are arranged now. For example, a good friend of mine works for the Continuing Education of the Bar. He runs their library. He is both an attorney and a librarian, and he is very much interested in the Librarians' Association, but as it stands right now and until adjustments are made in the bylaws he cannot belong.

The background out of which this organization has developed is, I think, very important. For the past two or three years there has been a lot of ferment among academic non-Senate employees of the University—mainly research workers, who outnumber the faculty, extension specialists, and librarians. All of these people have been defined by the University as academic, all recognize that they perform an academic function. None of them has any voice in the academic operation of the University. The only voice in academic affairs of the University which they have is through the administrative apparatus of which they are a part. Even without this kind of activity going on, I think that the University librarians would probably have done something. But it happened that at the time the Association was founded, two committees of the University were investigating the role of the non-Senate academic personnel—the President's committee called the Hoos Committee and the Academic Senate committee called the Spiess Committee. Both came out with recommendations providing more voice for academic employees, some form of security of employment, grievance procedures, and this kind of thing. Consequently, when the librarians met together at the 1967 ALA Conference in San Francisco, the natural focus of their goals tended to be these committees and a general awareness that there was a place for them to deal with matters of concern to them *within* the University structure; moreover, that this place be created in the academic structure. So the

Association as it has grown and as we have formed it ourselves, establishing its structure and bylaws, has been patterned very consciously after the Academic Senate, with chapters on the campuses, a state-wide assembly, and similar kinds of committees, only concerned with library problems. That's it in capsule form. The Association has been in operation since the beginning of this year.

Have you made up any recommendations of any kind?

Well, right now our major effort is to develop a proposal for official recognition, to be presented to the University before the end of the year. We have explored this somewhat. There is a serious problem as to whether the University will want to recognize a separate librarian's association. I know the administration would like to have a broader organization that would include the research workers and others. But the librarians do not want this for the very reason that the Academic Senate doesn't want to open its doors to the research workers. Members of the Senate feel that they would be deluged and that the Senate's orientation might shift, say from educational concerns to research concerns, or from classroom to laboratory concerns, perhaps, a little too much. Or I think mainly the Senate doesn't quite know what would happen. They have felt that the researchers and other academic non-Senate categories should have a separate organization parallel to the Senate. For the same reason, we believe that the University should be consistent and have a separate organization for each different academic group, recognizing that the librarians are essentially concerned with library problems of an academic nature, extension specialists with their own problems, and research workers with their particular problems. Any group that includes the research workers will be inundated by them and by their concerns.

I infer from this that you would like to develop a separate library organization on the campus. Is this a matter of preference or because you haven't been able to climb under the umbrella of the faculty senate?

There are arguments pro and con—and I can see them I think—but my personal feeling at the moment is that in long-range terms it is best for librarians to have their own organization. What I should like to see, and I think that this is the general direction in which things are ultimately going to have to move, are separate organizations for each of the academic groups, including librarians, all of which come together in a general academic assembly where they concern themselves with the overall academic issues that touch everyone. My feeling is that libraries are becoming more complex, that the caliber of librarians generally is rising, that the demands placed on librarians are increasing and that there are more and more specialists functioning in the library who have to be given their heads. For example, if the University brings someone in, as we have done here recently, to develop a Near Eastern collection in Hebrew, Yiddish, and the Arabic languages, who is competent to evaluate the collection he builds except the man himself, or perhaps he in conjunction with the appropriate faculty? And the faculty are not knowledgeable in terms of the bibliographical, book trade, and library problems. These are the library specialist's area and he is the only person qualified to make decisions. We have a Slavic specialist in the same situation.

Are these librarians?

These are both librarians.

With special language ability?

That's right—and with special bibliographical skills and backgrounds.

What you're saying then is that libraries are growing more complex, more specialized; therefore in the long run it will be better if the librarians on the campus are recognized officially as a separate professional group, but with representation in a broader group.

Right, and perhaps that we should have joint committees of faculty-librarians concerned with certain problems such as long-range curricular planning, adequate financial provision for library purposes before new procedure programs are approved, and the like. I think one of the difficulties frequently encountered in an academic institution in such planning is that the librarians are not sufficiently involved, particularly in a large institution like this where one has to call on specialists. In other words, the top administrator cannot really judge if a Slavic collection is good or not—he has to depend on the specialist. So the Slavic librarian-specialist really should be directly involved in long-range planning, not just by the Slavic department faculty, but by the political scientists and sociologists and others who have Slavic research concerns.

This makes a great deal of sense to me. One problem I see is that the kind of close relationship the librarian needs in order to become involved academically with the faculty may come naturally to the Slavic specialist and to others simply because they are specialists working closely with a faculty who is dependent on them. But there are not many jobs of this kind in a university library. The vast majority of librarians are still needed to order, catalog, and service books. Does this mean splitting a library staff into two kinds of librarians?

I suppose you really mean the management people, or the operations people as opposed to the subject specialists.

Yes, but perhaps I could put it this way. Are you building your case on too limited a number of library specialists?

Well, I've thought a good deal about this. It seems to me that the only basis now for justifying the employment of librarians with an advanced education in a university system is on one or another kind of specialty. From the point of view of the special nature of the material and a command of the bibliography rather than from the point of view of subject interest *per se*, I think that a librarian who manages a government publications collection is as much a specialist as one who is building a Slavic collection; the same is true of a librarian who manages a map collection. Or take my own field, someone who is involved in organizing and managing out-of-print acquisitions. This person has to be a specialist in a particular area or in a particular kind of process, a particular kind of material. One who manages out-of-print acquisitions has to know the antiquarian book trade, the way it works. Someone who manages documents has to know documents and the kinds of agencies that they come from, and what their peculiarities and uses are. To function well in such a capacity, a librarian must have specialized graduate education in the bibliographical control and operations of his field as well as several years experience in his particular specialty. I think that this is the direction that librarianship is going to have to take. It is really the answer to an old problem that has plagued us for years: the differentiation of the professional from the nonprofessional. I think that present stress and strain—increased publication, increased demand—is indicating those areas which are truly professional. And like other professions, this means specialization.

The state college librarians have something going of this kind. Do you think it is better for the university librarians to work these things out separately or should they combine with the state college people?

Well, I think there are certain differences. There are differences say between a research library and a library that is mainly supporting teaching. However, in colleges—and universities, too —librarians should take a stronger educational role. I think the need is a part of the growing complexity of publication and research. Just take reference materials for example; every year there are many more bibliographies published. It is not easy anymore for even an advanced academic person—a graduate student or faculty member—to find his way around in the literature of a field with which he is not intimately acquainted. And I think that all these difficulties make it more and more incumbent on most librarians in the colleges and universities to play a strong educational role, probably right in the classroom. There is an experimental program starting here, in which I have been involved, for an undergraduate course in the use of the library to be taught by librarians. It will begin in late September and carry on throughout the year. It is part of the curriculum of the experimental college of the University. I know this type of instruction has had ups and downs and that there is nothing new about such a course, but it seems to me that there is a whole new interest arising again in this kind of instruction in many colleges and that the need for it is greater than ever.

Basically, you appear to be saying that the state colleges have different problems from the university and that the librarians of each must solve their problems of status separately.

In the university library as distinguished from the college, there is a greater need for librarians who are keyed to research, who can coordinate and develop complex research collections. College and university librarians also share many problems—

the educational role of the librarian, upgrading reference service, and so forth.

What kind of preparation in the library schools will produce librarians who have subject, linguistic, and bibliographical training combined? I do not see the present graduates as being any more specialized in their qualifications than those of ten or twenty years ago.

I think this is a problem the library schools have to solve. They seem to have been debating for the last thirty years or more whether they should train the generalist or the specialist. My feeling is that it is more and more incumbent upon them to prepare the specialist and that they should have faced up to this long ago. And I don't mean just specialists for the university library. It seems to me that the public libraries now demand a different kind of specialist. Take the problem of the public library within a ghetto community. Urban libraries are more and more centered in such communities and there's a whole dynamic program, a very exciting program, developing out of this with a much more community-oriented and community-conscious approach to the patron. I saw an article in the San Francisco *Chronicle* the other day about the librarians in San Francisco, who were taking their books out into the ghetto and laying them out on the hoods of their cars for passers by to see, in an attempt to get them to read and to use the libraries. So it seems to me that the schools have to prepare this type of librarian. They may need to shift away from the old routine and perhaps doctrinaire approach to cataloging and acquisition and other basic courses. I am not suggesting that these courses should be eliminated, but that they should be taken more quickly and in a more theoretical fashion, assuming that the necessary training will be picked up on the job anyway. I think that library school education should be devoted to more specialized instruction, particularly during the second semester, so that it produces the kinds of librarians that are desperately needed by today's society—public librarians with a real sociological and educational orientation; subject specialists who have a genuine bibliographical command of their specialties; specialists in maps or technical reports or government publications who know the perculiarities and bibliographical intricacies of these materials; academic librarians with the knowledge

and skill to give meaningful instruction in library use and research techniques.

*There are special course programs for medical librarians, law
librarians, and the like. Perhaps the special kind of preparation
could be custom designed to fill the need?*

I have just been reading the symposium in the *Journal of
Library Education* on the programs in our library schools. One
of the things that keeps popping up in the articles concerns the
training of specialists in a one-year period beyond the master's
degree for which some schools are now giving certificates.
This seems to be a possible answer, although I think that the
basic MLS program should be overhauled as well.

*Could this training be given outside the library school where
more subject or language training is needed?*

I think that it should be kept within the library school, but
with some strong orientation toward a subject or materials
specialty or a strong emphasis on management courses for
the administrator. This seems to me to be a very sensible approach. It has its parallel in medicine. The medical student first
gets his general M.D. degree and then comes back to study
his specialty after a period of internship. I think this might
be a useful procedure for librarians. I am not convinced that
the Ph.D. is really that necessary or important for librarians, but
some kind of specialty beyond the master's degree might be very
important.

*In times like these when there is a great emphasis on con-
temporary relevance, how does the university library make its
contribution? Departments, of course, offer special courses in
urban problems, black power, and the like.*

Up to now at least, I think that it has been on a rather informal basis. I have friends on the staff who make contributions.
The librarian in charge of the development of the undergraduate
library collection here has associated herself with one of the
Oakland youth programs under the sponsorship of the University
and is working with the program on the development of a
working collection. She does this on her own time. She is developing a bibliography for them; when this is completed, she
will help buy and catalog the books and then assist in setting

up the library. And I know of other librarians who are doing the same thing. A good friend of mine at UCLA was involved in a similar project. But in answer to your question, I do not know of any formal way in which the university library or the library school has responded to this challenge. I must say there has been a real effort in library staffing to employ minority group members. But the kind of dynamic, information-oriented program a library might provide, I think has not yet been forthcoming here.

Do you think a university library can make such a contribution?

Yes, I think it can.

Do you have in mind, for example, that a university library might establish a special collection or set up an exhibit in the student union of books dealing with current problems?

One way might be to develop special collections and make them available. There is a project going on here that is related to this. The University Library is making a real effort to develop a collection of minority publications which involves the literature of all the local groups—the hand-outs, suitable background literature, etc. There is an effort going on under our new librarian, responding to proposals made by certain staff members, to have a student advisory committee with representation from minority group students. If such a committee were developed, I think perhaps it could suggest the kinds of programs which are needed and the library in turn would come up with the kinds of response it can make.

Do you think there are other ways in which libraries can respond to the student movement, minority problems of the day?

I think so, particularly over a period of time. I think this is all a new kind of experience, particularly with most of us as well as with most students. And you have to develop something in the way of a tradition or an *esprit* in which this is a creative experience in involvement and not just a response to a student political move. This goes back to the need for more dynamic and vital librarians, which an emphasis on specialization would encourage.

Would it be helpful to have a student library representative on the faculty library committee?

I think it would be good. As a matter of fact, I think the library should attempt to make a strong tie to the whole university community, even the general community outside the campus. Which means that there is not simply a faculty advisory group but a dynamic student library committee as well, and some kind of contact with the other groups which we have been talking about, the academic non-Senate groups and the nonacademic groups, so that they can all be involved in what the library does and make the kind of suggestions which can make a library more vital to them and to the whole community. Up to now, so far as I know, the only library committee the University has had is a faculty committee of the University Senate. It has not been terribly dynamic.

Well, I guess that is about par for the course. The word "dynamic" is a good word; the problem is how to develop dynamism. The student library committee, for example, is a good idea if it has the right staff leadership. How do you get it?

It could be one of the functions of the undergraduate librarian, the librarian in charge of the new undergraduate library here. I see that job as a crucial public relations job. It needs a librarian with educational and library development leadership.

Let me ask you about another matter. I have recently read a long list of demands by the local professional librarian's union to the new director of libraries. There is nothing confidential about it; it was widely distributed to the colonies. What you have just described as the function of your association of professional librarians makes a lot of sense to me. But a union sets up an adversary and might that defeat one of the major objectives you have—if academic involvement is a major aim?

I agree with what you say. There is no question that a union is an adversary organization. Its whole thrust and force is geared to that kind of relationship. Its tools are pressure and strikes. It depends, however, upon the kind of situation in which you find yourself. If you can work in consort with the library and university administration, where you can get more than just an informal commitment based on moment-to-moment good will of the parties involved, then it seems to me that a union may be unnecessary. The union developed at Berkeley because we had, in fact, an adversary situation, not simply within the library but within the University as a whole. I think the professional librarians' association would never have gotten started had it not been for union activity. Unions were a threat to the University which the administration didn't want to see spread, particularly the librarian's union, which was very active. It bothered and worried the University. I think that if the goals of librarians— the real goals and their problems—can be reached and solved through a less antagonistic organization, then I'm all for it. The whole matter of the professional union is an open question. It's a muddy problem at best. No one really knows how to proceed. Most of the professional unions are relatively new— even the teachers' union. They really haven't worked out exactly what organized labor is going to do for them, what their commitments to organized labor involve. That's been a tough problem for us and it has drawn us into situations which I believe are not always in our best interests. If I were to write my article on library unions over again, I would probably do it differently, I think, based on later experience. I still think that in that particular situation and at that particular time, it was correct to organize the union. I think also that the union has played a very strong role in professionalizing librarians here, bringing them together, making them more conscious of professional goals, but I am much more skeptical now of what its long-range goal can be. I think that perhaps a union is, more than anything else, an indication that things have just gotten out of hand and that the whole situation has to be re-evaluated. I think that we're particularly fortunate in having a new librarian come in at this particular time, who is, himself, forced to look at things afresh, and who, I think, represents a somewhat different philosophy and will perhaps work with us on achieving a more cooperative solution.

You wrote something about your experiences at the Kansas ALA meeting in the latest CU newsletter. (CU is the title of the University of California Library's [Berkeley] newsletter.) You seemed to me to see a split between two types or kinds of librarians as expressed in the council and meetings you attended. Could you expand on this a bit?

I think it was basically a philosophical difference; perhaps a lot of it was a matter of generation. I don't know if someone like Ralph Blasingame would be called a new or old librarian—to my way of thinking he is an old librarian. Yet he seemed to me to be one of the better spokesmen for the anti-establishment. That's really what I think it is—pro-establishment and anti-establishment. And this is why I asked you before we started the tape what you felt was the dominant characteristic of the librarians, say of your generation. Now I've been thinking a lot about this since we had lunch because you raised this point then and it intrigued me. And while I must admit that my ignorance about this is monumental, it seems to me that perhaps the major thrust of the librarians between 1900 and 1945 or 1950 was operational or organizational, bringing good management into the library, setting up the libraries. The collections began to get big. It became obvious that two or three people could not run them on a kind of hit-or miss, helter-skelter basis, and do their scholarly work at the same time. So they had to bring in full-time librarians who were geared to making the collections available. It was during this period that the basic acquisitions and circulation routines were set up and all the related functions of library work. It seems to me that this is perhaps the dominant characteristic of this period. Most of these procedures were modeled, as one would expect, on business practices as applied to the library. Perhaps this was the best answer at the time because the problem was to set up the libraries and get them operational.

Now I think with the complexity and breadth of publication that's arisen since World War II, and with the tremendous developments in research and the changes in population that are taking place, the need is for more and more specialists in the libraries. The procedures set up in the earlier generation seem to be yielding to automation of one kind or another. The real tight bibliographical control, the documentalist, the specialist, the community worker in public libraries, this is the direction for the young librarians today. I think that part of what went on at the ALA meeting was a conflict between these two groups. To me, the whole conference was summed up in one meeting which actually did not attract a great deal of press notice, although it was very well attended. It was concerned with the bibliographer in the academic library. Two very different—in fact, opposed—views were presented. The main speaker and one respondent argued that the bibliographer must be a specialist, that he must develop the collections, work with the faculty, know the antiquarian trade, and have a real subject background to be successful.

The other respondent contended that this was all well and good, but that the real role of the bibliographer was to check the trade information accurately, make sure there was no duplication, establish the main entry, etc., and there, I thought, was the real confrontation of the new and the old librarian.

Maurice F. Tauber

In May, 1968, Findlay College, Ohio, awarded its Distinguished Service Award to Dr. Maurice F. Tauber for "outstanding contributions to higher education, as a teacher, writer, librarian, critic, and leader in the science of library service and 'partner in learning' to untold numbers." It was a fitting tribute and accurate characterization of a man whose universal cast of mind and warm personality are widely recognized and applauded. Educated at Temple, Columbia, and Chicago universities, he has served all three as librarian in one position or another but none for a longer period of time and with greater distinction than Columbia, where he was named Melvil Dewey Professor of Library Service in 1954. Robert Downs summed up Dr. Tauber's accomplishments on the occasion of his retirement from fourteen years of editorship of *College and Research Libraries* in these words: "Viewing his numerous commitments as an author, editor, teacher, lecturer, and consultant, it seems all the more astonishing that Maurice Tauber could have found time for the demanding duties of editing a leading professional journal. The fact that he performed that function with distinction while carrying a multitude of other activities is a tribute not only to his industry but also to his ability to budget his time, his talent for organization, and dedication to his profession."

Dr. Tauber was interviewed at Emory University in the spring of 1968.

The last time we were together you were emceeing a conference on library surveys.* You and Irlene Stephens edited the proceedings of that conference. How did the book sell?

Fine, the first edition sold out.

We are a bit given to fads in this country and this is discernible in librarianship. I wondered at the time of the conference if the survey craze had reached its peak?

No, I do not think there has been any dimunition in survey activity; it is steady and constant. I get calls for survey help every week which I direct to other people simply because I do not have time for them. Mark Gormley and I have just finished one at Kenyon College in Ohio.

Do you think there is still a real need for surveys? What is the survey's main contribution?

In academic institutions there are presidents, vice-presidents, deans, and department heads, and in public libraries boards of trustees, directors of the library, and other supervisory officers who are not willing to make decisions—surgical decisions—to uproot a library in order to get something done. They need outside consultants to come in to tell them what they have to do. There are any number of institutions in this country— public, academic, and special—where the library administration has been an obstacle to getting things done. With the aid of a consultant, the supervisory authority seeks to get rid of the librarian and to find a new one. There are too many assignments of this kind, what a colleague of mine and I call the "iceberg assignment." The president or board brings you in for one thing, but what they really want is to fire somebody. Recently I have made a practice of asking such questions as these: "Is there somebody who has to be fired? Is there an administrative decision which you should make on the basis of known evidence, to which nobody could add no matter how long he consulted with you?" If there is, the president or board should make the decision and not bother with a consultant.

---

*The Conference on Library Surveys was held at Columbia University, June 14-17, 1965, and the proceedings of the Institute were published in Maurice F. Tauber and Irlene R. Stephens, eds., *Library Surveys*. New York: Columbia University Press, 1967.

Surveys represent a contribution to the national bank of information that we have accumulated. Some of them seem to be repetitious—as one reviewer stated "merely a change of a name here and there"—but to tell the truth every library is different. There is not a one where the same prescription would fit. Surveys represent an approach to specific library problems which require very detailed analysis in respect to recommendations that are made for changes or improvements. It is not possible to make such recommendations without the complete cooperation of the library staff and the experience of the surveyors to outline steps that ought to be taken in regard to the development of the particular library service.

The failures in library development may be correlated completely with the ineptitude on the part of library administrators to make forceful decisions that are important for furthering the progress of library development.

In your experience as a surveyor, I am sure you have dealt with many problems besides the "iceberg assignment" to which you have referred. What about the question of reclassification?

If you have used seven Dewey classification editions and you can't use the Dewey numbers on cards, you are growing at a rate faster than you can handle the material. You either have to reclassify according to the latest edition of Dewey or else change to the Library of Congress classification. This is one of the basic problems throughout the country. It is not a question, really, as Robert Downs sometimes says, of wasting money. You waste money as long as you continue using a classification which requires custom-tailored applications. It takes almost fifteen minutes to half an hour to classify a book, and you are still not certain of what the product is. It is a waste of time and it can only get worse.

What other problems have you encountered in your survey work?

In cataloging, failure to use centralized services from the Library of Congress, modifying the entries, and altering the subject headings to the extent that it becomes almost a "tailor-made" business. We used to emphasize in library school that every library is different up to a certain point. But the similarity between libraries is greater than their differences. We talk so much about methods to handle certain things that can be centralized and accomplished through a cooperative enterprise, and then there are individualists in catalog departments who feel that they know better. What they do is to create a situation which, over a long period of time, is so unique and so different that centralized services really cannot be applied.

In some instances there is pressure from the faculty members for the kind of special classification modifications of which you speak. Changes may be made because the catalogers do not always get the backing of the librarian.

That's right! Another point that we sometimes find in surveys is the inefficient use of personnel. When I go to a library and the librarian tells me that it's all right to have eight catalogers and two clerks in his catalog department, I'm ready to have a heart attack. Even a superficial study of the department shows that the ratio of professional to clerical should be more nearly the reverse. So I say to the librarian that this is a problem he should do something about. "I have more important problems—personnel problems," he replies. To which the only answer is, "You surely do, and this is one of your most important ones. You can shift four professionals to other staff assignments almost immediately if you reorganize your department." Well, it was done in that particular library, but so often one meets up with this failure to use clerical people for nonprofessional tasks with the result that the library wastes money all along the line. We have not utilized clerical and technical assistants in the library to a point where the professionals can really spend their time on the important things.

But we have made progress in that direction. Wouldn't a study of the professional-clerical ratio today and ten years ago show a definite swing to the kind of staffing you are recommending?

That's right.

A minute ago you mentioned the practice of bringing in a consultant to effect a dismissal. Is this a frequent occurrence?

I'm afraid that it is.

Do you think that the situation really requires separation or is there simply a lack of communication between the trustees or administrator and the librarian?

That's partly involved, but usually the evidence about a situation of this sort represents not merely the views of the administrator—president, provost, or other administrator—but the accumulation of evidence from faculty members, student groups, and members of the staff, especially the supervisory staff. Unless it is a civil service case, which may be a little complex, the librarian is usually moved, transferred, or dismissed. This is happening constantly in libraries, to a greater extent in the last half-dozen years than ever before. I believe administrative officers in libraries have come to the conclusion that in order to get a job done one must be forthright in making a decision about a person who fails to meet expectations—a personality problem, absenteeism, what you might call deterioration in a position in which he is no longer effective. These people are being moved out and I don't think that this is wrong. Most librarians are humane, which is one of the reasons they have retained people in posts far longer than they should. We don't want to hurt people. I believe it is so important to identify the point of no return with respect to an individual in meeting the tremendous pressures under which libraries now operate that administrators are becoming a little tougher. Also I believe that other members of the staff in a particular situation do not accept the idea of retaining an ineffective supervisor.

Science and technology are having a strong impact on library operations. Have they affected your curriculum in the library school and the kind of students you are recruiting?

On the whole I would say that a very large proportion of the students who are coming to library school are very much interested in the application of automation to librarianship. We have at Columbia introduced in the last few years a course on information systems and an advanced seminar on information systems.* Within the framework of this nucleus of courses, Columbia has introduced a new course on indexing and abstracting which incorporates such mechanization and utilization

---

*Special course offerings: "Seminar in the Theory of Information Control," and "Modern Information Systems."

as is appropriate. I think these represent some of the pressure points in terms of library needs. The application of this course work is not limited to science and technology; it extends to the social sciences and even to the humanities. There is a group in New York University, working with the American Council on Learned Societies, which is interested in the computerization of information in literature. We have pressure from students, rather than from anyone else, to be aware and alert to the particular potentials of technology.

Is there a danger that the current emphasis on technology may lead to students being more interested in mechanics than in books and reading?

I don't think so. Lawrence Powell, who represents the epitome of bookish librarianship, was responsible for bringing Robert Hayes* to the University of California at Los Angeles to set up an information program in the library school. I would hope that we would not turn out what I would call unbalanced librarians. I do not believe this interest in automation has made us at Columbia any less interested in turning out librarians who are competent across-the-board in the areas of the humanities and social sciences. On the other hand, I think library service has become more complex; there is a greater degree of specialization than when you and I went to library school. I see nothing wrong in this. Lehigh, Georgia Tech, and other institutions, which have introduced so-called courses of information science, are somewhat different from those provided in the traditional library school. As a matter of fact, they represent a different breed. I am still not sure what the University of Chicago has done at this point. It might be worth while for Don Swanson to tell the profession what has been accomplished in Chicago's particular program. It would be interesting, perhaps, to have some of these information science schools indicate what they are doing and in what way they have improved upon the standards of the more conventional library school curriculum. I do not believe that we have yet had follow-ups on graduates of these programs. By this I mean that I do not think we have the evidence which would give us a basis for making a clear-cut

---

*Professor, UCLA School of Library Service, 1964-to date. Library systems analyst and director of the Institute of Library Research.

distinction as to their contribution as against that of the so-called traditional library school. I would say that most of the typical schools have introduced one or two courses in information science, automation, and computerization. Sometimes these are coordinated with the computer center on the campus. At Columbia, students can take courses without charge in elementary computer information. They can take a six-week course for nothing. Library school students are registering for these courses. It is almost like mathematics, language, or any other skill course, a necessary attribute for getting along.

What is the nature of this six-week course? Do students get practical experience? Do they have to take a refresher course in mathematics to take the computer course?

With respect to the six-week course, I should say a few words about the computers and the School of Library Service. The Computer Center of the University offers a self-teaching (programmed manual) course introducing EAM (punched card) equipment, together with some information on computers. This is hands-on experience, including the keypunchers, sorter, 407, reproducing punch, and so on. The student punches a small program, including job cards, which is given in the manual, and runs it to learn Center procedures.

In regard to other courses at the Computer Center and in the School of Library Service, the programming courses, which are different, teach specific programming languages. The student submits his own programs from the first day on, and at least one language is taught each semester with bibliographic examples. Nothing suitable is offered in the summer; so Dr. Hines teaches a programming course for School of Library Service students; this is done with the consent of the Center.

There is also a course in "Computing and Libraries," taught by Dr. Michael Barnett of RCA, who is developing (and teaches, with runs by students) a language especially suited to library procedures or problems. In the indexing course, students punch entry cards for a book indexing program and run it. It is hoped that by next fall, for the Information Systems course, there will be developed KWIC, KWOC, enriched KWOC, and Wilson-type indexes.

No mathematical knowledge or ability is required for these courses, or for bibliographic programming in general.

What is your approach to automation in your own courses?

My feeling about our program at Columbia is that rather than go off into a high-powered curriculum in automation systems as such, we try to blend it with what we have. The course in technical services dealing with acquisitions, cataloging, or organization, and conservation of materials will bring in current developments. This is attempted. The most recent readings are always assigned. The latest information which appears to have some potential is always brought to the attention of the student—the MARC project of the Library of Congress, the cooperative study project now underway at Columbia, Stanford, and Chicago, and so forth. The critical thing at this point is for the librarian to watch these new developments. The results of the projects I have mentioned have implications for all major research librarians in the country.

Has the free speech movement in the universities of this state had any significant impact on libraries and librarians?

I wish I could say that it had affected the library. I do not see any real effect. I think it has shaken up curricular thinking and the older hidebound generation of teachers in universities, perhaps in good ways. On the other hand, I am afraid that in some instances it has been overplayed as at Columbia, and it may be a long time before Columbia regains its equilibrium. For what it is worth, and I am surely no judge, I believe this unrest has peaked, perhaps. I think the brutality of the Columbia incident, burning of the president's office at Stanford, really shocked students as well as their seniors, and one would hope that nothing quite so violent will happen again unless universities slide back into despondency.

At Columbia, as a result of the student strikes, there was some effort on the part of the nonprofessional staff to reactivate a staff association and to seek participation in some phases of library administration.

Do you regard this effort as beneficial or detrimental to the library?

I think the primary short-term interest was to raise salaries and secure shorter hours. But in terms of what is potentially possible by greater staff participation in policy and administration, we have not experimented sufficiently to make a judgment. I think certain institutions have potentials which probably do not exist in other institutions. I think this is something that ought to be studied on an individual library basis. In a place like New York which has a good union history, there is a strong union tendency. It is very difficult for certain people to realize that they are not allowed to be members of a union because they are employees of a private institution.

Are there unions at Columbia?

Yes, there are unions for the janitorial staff, elevator operators, and others. Some members of the staff belong to a union. On the basis of the student demonstrations at Columbia and the renewed interest in the nonacademic staff of the library in personnel matters, I think there is a good possibility that there will be coordinated efforts to improve not only the conditions of hours, salaries, and special privileges, but also to seek more opportunity for career positions for the nonprofessional. This is one of the things that needs attention. There are many such positions in cataloging, circulation, binding, and in other departments. The persons who work here are a floating group. They come for two or three years only.

Do you think the movement toward unions would help to stabilize employment at these levels?

Yes, I do. If you belong to a plumber's union or some other trade, you do not expect to shift from one type of work to another. You train for one trade and stick with it. The turnover in clerical workers in the library, on the other hand is, overwhelming. Many work in the same position or library less than a year.

Robert G. Vosper

THE name is arresting, like the personality for which it stands. A photograph of Robert Vosper holding a bottle of Old Library bourbon, unveiled on the occasion of a banquet of the Franklin D. Murphy Associates of UCLA when he was named Man of the Year, reveals something of the essential man—his magnanimity and largeness of spirit and his warm humanity.

Robert Vosper was born in Portland, Oregon, in 1913. He earned the B.A. (1937) and M.A. 1939 in Classics) from the University of Oregon, and his library degree from the University of California, Berkeley (1940). He served as president of the Association of College and Research Libraries in 1956-1957, and as president of the American Library Association in 1965-1966. He has held Fulbright and Guggenheim fellowships for study and research in Europe.

When Vosper became head librarian of the University of Kansas in 1952, he immediately established himself as a university librarian of unusual ability and originality, one whose work had to a marked degree the Midas touch. At the University of California at Los Angeles, where he succeeded Lawrence Clark Powell as University Librarian and Professor of Library Science, he not only repeated earlier successes but extended them.

The interview took place in the summer of 1968 at his office in the new research library of UCLA.

A recent development in academic library history is the assumption by the librarian of a much greater responsibility for book selection than in the past, when most libraries looked to the faculty to generate the book orders. How has this come about? What is the explanation?

Actually, I think this is one of the really interesting and creative changes in the library structure in this country and it has come about pretty much since World War II, increasingly in the last ten years or so. At the time Perry Danton wrote that wonderful book on book selection* in German and American university libraries, it was clear that over the long haul the experience you mention was a fairly typical one in this country. The faculty did 80 percent of the book selection on the theory that they were the experts and they knew; the library staff filled in the interstices, reference books, and so on. This was true here almost entirely up until and into the 1950's, when it began to change. During the years I was at the University of Kansas, we were working on the Farmington plan** and the Association of Research Libraries asked me to undertake a review of the whole Farmington plan structure. I went around the country and talked to everybody about how they selected books, what they did. Except in a few cases selection by the faculty was the normal pattern. In those days—this was in the 1950's—Harvard had a small pool of book selection people in the library who worked with Ed Williams. There was another small group at Michigan; that was about it. Now today, as you say, at UCLA, Indiana, Stanford and, increasingly around the country, the large libraries have full-time specialist book selection people. I think a number of things have brought about this change. One is that the amount of publication has gotten so large and increased so rapidly that our faculty cannot keep up with it in the way they could in an earlier day. Library book collections have become larger and more complex. The faculty cannot keep in touch with what is and what isn't in the library in the way they could in an age when the library was smaller. Furthermore, in many of these

---

Book Selection and Collection. New York: Columbia University Press, 1963.
**Farmington plan had as its purpose the acquisition of at least one copy of all foreign publications relevant for research by American university libraries.

places, the faculty do not remain with the institution in the way they did in the 1930's and 1940's when a man would come in as an assistant professor and remain. He had a really intimate tie with the situation and developed a sense of institutional loyalty which is now lacking. Now the faculty come and go; they are off on sabbatical, on government projects, and they move from one institution to another. It takes a long time at one institution to build up enough knowledge and detail of the library collection to acquire books for it. The faculty do not have it anymore. And then they are busier now than they used to be. Academic life here in the 1940's was fairly comfortable. The faculty had a fair amount of time. Now they are pushed from pillar to post on research contracts, review boards; they are frequently on leave to the federal government and they all have to publish. Life is busier; they move at a faster pace. They just do not have the time for book selection which they once had. The spread of interdisciplinary research has been influential also. An increasing amount of literature is peripheral to several disciplines and the responsibility of no one department. I think another major factor has been the impact of the foreign area studies program, which is of course basically interdisciplinary, pushing libraries to get books from all over the world. And this just added to the complexity of the task because these materials are not conveniently reviewed in the subject reviewing journals. So the faculty could not deal with the problem anymore and did not want to. At the same time, a young generation of librarians coming along was interested and began to develop the right kind of competence. I think these are some of the factors.

If a university acquires for itself a point of distinction—Far Eastern studies, space study, a center for Oriental art—its library usually reflects the interests and idiosyncrasies of its distinguished faculty who have developed these collections. Is there not a danger that the shift to library bibliographer selection will result in standardization and less distinction?

I am sure what you say has always been true in the past, but increasingly in the future it will be the idiosyncrasies of skilled librarians, perhaps, which will bring distinction to our collections. I do not think of the result of the bibliographer's efforts as following a standardized pattern because these people, these subject specialists, are an arm of the library working in close relation with the faculty. They will respond to the same kinds of requirements and needs and idiosyncracies that the academic institution has for teaching and research. I think they will do a better job than the faculty did in the past, but I do not think this will necessarily result in a standardized list of best books. Each book selector will have a different understanding of needs as will each institution.

Has the trend toward blanket orders come along with the subject bibliographer program?

Yes, I think the two have come along in parallel, and for somewhat similar reasons. They developed at the same time because the mass of books from which we need to buy has become so large and the pace of research so rapid that we have to get the books faster. We are constantly looking for mechanisms to speed up the whole intake process. And the blanket order is one way to select quickly from the current output. For example, in retrospective buying our bibliographers are concerned mainly with selection on a title-by-title basis. They comb the antiquarian catalogues, they go to Europe, Africa, Latin America, and buy in the field. The current books come in on blanket orders so the bibliographers do not have to select them book by book, which is a long slow process. But they monitor the intake. Books come in and they look them over and compare them with what they think we ought to have and they say we shouldn't be getting this or we ought to be getting that. The selection is under rational control but it is handled in a more expeditious and faster way. It is partly a result of the number of books being published, the lack of adequate bibliography in certain countries, and the need to get the material rapidly. The classical attitude toward book selection, what the German librarian and professor practice as Danton says in his book, regards the selection of the individual book as the intellectual problem. You build a library book by book; you get only the best books in each scholarly field. I look on book selection, and I think many of us tend to, as a selection of fields, a selection of emphases, but not as a selection of individual books because the research man, in historical and comparative fields, needs to review good books and bad books, major books and minor background books in quantity. In this I except, of course, such fields as science and engineering.

You are not concerned that a blanket order brings in all the books reviewed, let us say, in the American Historical Review, *including a large number which are described as repetitious and worthless?*

No, I don't think so. It seems to me that our graduate students and faculty ought to have a chance to decide for themselves whether a book is useful or significant. I do not think that the reviewer's opinion is important in those terms—building a library for all times and providing a view of social history.

Are these new developments in university library book selection and acquisition confined to the major research libraries?

Yes, I suppose so. I cannot speak out of experience for collegiate institutions or smaller universities, but certainly this is the tempo and style of the big complex university library in the 1960's and 1970's. It's a whole new style of life. Tremendously exciting, you know! The librarians I really envy deep down in my green heart these days are those youngsters who have full-time jobs as book selection officers. If I were just smart enough and young enough to be the person who does nothing but buy books in support of medieval and renaissance studies at UCLA, it would be wonderful. Go off to Europe to visit the book shops, buy books, spend money, and not have to do anything else. I would spend my time talking to faculty and graduate students to learn what they need. It's a beautiful job, but you have to know something to do it, more than I ever knew as a book selector. You must have a real knowledge of books, not just a vague love of books.

Does this new trend add to the cost of acquiring books?

Oh, I'm sure it adds to the cost. You save certain kinds of clerical costs when you don't buy book by book, you know. On the other hand the brains required for selection are expensive brains if they are any good, so I just assume that the cost goes up. And I think as a consequence the product is better.

Are these bibliographers all librarians?

By and large the ideal person, and you see it here, is somebody who has been trained as a librarian but who has also at least an M.A. in a relevant subject field—Middle Eastern studies, African studies, medieval studies, whatever it might be, plus real linguistic competence so that the bibliographer can go off to the Far East or to Eastern Europe or to Western Europe and talk to booksellers and buy books, immediately at first hand. Now, in a few cases we have brought in people who have a Ph.D. plus library training. This is the high ideal almost. Our Near Eastern studies bibliographer has a Ph.D. in Egyptology and is a graduate of our Graduate Library School, could teach just as well as be a librarian, and is competent in both directions as a productive research person. She is a pre-eminent type. Sometimes we've slipped over the other way—we are bringing in a Latin American bibliographer who is just finishing a Ph.D. in Latin American studies. He has a bookish-bibliographical bent. We have encouraged him to come as our Latin American bibliographer, to start library school, and to pick up a library degree on top of his Ph.D., If this all works out, he also could be the best kind. You need both types of training. But in this day and age, it is difficult to get both.

Is it hard to retain these men for bibliographical work? Do they have leanings toward teaching?

Well, I think it is good that in some cases they do and it's a matter of trying to work an effective balance between the two. I am pleased when, for example, our Near Eastern bibliographer or our Hebrew bibliographer both teach part time. They do not try to teach full time or even half time, but they teach a course. The Near Eastern bibliographer teaches a course in Egyptology in the history department. The Hebrew bibliographer gives a course in research method and bibliography. Our Oriental librarian gives a course in bibliographical method in the department of Oriental languages. This kind of teaching, I think, is very good. And it means the bibliographers have an academic appointment in a department and have the status of a real colleague. They know the library problem the teacher faces, and I think a lot of us in libraries miss that. We do not understand what the hell the poor teacher is complaining about. When you teach you begin to see that the library is often a bloody nuisance. So I think, if you can balance this, teaching is a good thing. Indeed, what we face with these people is that they have real academic know-how and real academic aspirations. The library has to offer them a career that is as creative and full of future as a full-time teaching career in a university.

You have to provide them with travel money, with research opportunity—the academic life, somehow.

How do you balance these kind of privileges with those afforded other members of the staff who are organizing and making the material available?

I think that the professional staff need to have access to something like a sabbatical leave—that is, opportunity for refreshment and further study within their own field of competence. I think this is terribly important if you are calling on people to remain intellectually alive and to keep in touch with a subject field as well as with librarianship, which is changing rapidly today. Otherwise you build, as we have in the past, a lot of old-timers who went to library school twenty years ago and who are competent craftsmen but who haven't been re-energized. So I think something like a sabbatical leave is very important. Industry is learning this. Academic institutions knew it a long time ago. Librarians need it for the same reason, I think. If you have these kinds of persons they need access to research funds and travel funds. And they need to be in an environment in which they feel a sense of real participation with the teaching and research staff in the development of the university. In some institutions this means that they ought to be represented in the academic senate—these things vary from institution to institution—but they need to have a sense of sharing in the academic enterprise. In other institutions it may mean mechanical things, like membership in a faculty club, but it also involves a much more intellectual aspect of involvement and discussion of university policy.

I also think that we are going to have to remake a lot of our administrative structure within the library. We are struggling with it at UCLA now so that there will be less of a sense of the hierarchical pattern of administration. As I look at our reference staff, they have to be scheduled so that the service will be maintained in the same way that professors have to be scheduled for class hours, but the tone, style, and objectives of the reference department can be developed and designed by the reference staff working together as an academic department works together. Not with a department head who sets all the style and pattern, but as a group of intellectually equal people, one of whom is *primus inter pares*. The same approach can be followed with a group of full-time book selection people. They have got to have the kind of flexibility to come and go as they see fit, to work with people on the campus, and to think about the end result of book selection throughout the university. Nobody can really tell them what to do. They have got to develop an intellectual ambience, participate in designing the end result of the library and academic structure. So there is this involvement too. I think these are the kinds of things—salary, yes, but involvement also.

The kind of situation you envisage for librarians would suggest the need for a strong back-up by a nonprofessional staff. One of the major problems of the university library is to provide stability and a career service in the nonprofessional positions. How are you meeting this problem at UCLA?

You ask this at an interesting time. At three o'clock Page Ackerman and I are going over to talk to the academic vice-chancellor and the chief of the personnel office on the campus about the whole matter of the structure of library staffing. We are looking toward working at the structure at two levels: one level is the one you have asked about and we are pretty clear about that. In order to do what I've been talking about, we have got to have a strong career support group who will increasingly take over the kind of thing old-fashioned professional librarians like myself did when we went into the library profession. More and more I think this has to be turned over to career-skilled, well-trained library assistants, library technicians, whatever terminology you use. We have come a ways in this direction in recent years. We are proposing now to move ahead a bit further and to develop a real career ladder for library assistants, with four gradations that will bring them in salary up to the middle of the professional grades. This proposal will offer a lifetime career, more or less, with people taking on important administrative tasks and a great deal of the fundamental processing effort.

Would you care to suggest what important administrative position a library assistant might achieve?

I can see, for example, one of these people being responsible for all cataloging with Library of Congress copy, in charge of the whole operation.

Do you think such a person might head up all circulation services?

I certainly think this is conceivable, particularly as we move into automated circulation mechanisms as we are now. Here a first-rate principal library assistant with systems experience could handle a circulation department, I'm sure.

The UC Voice *quoting you on the deplorable state of the professional librarian's treatment as compared with that of his teaching colleague, said that you considered such a matter "dangerous." Are you implying by this that you think a union organization in academic librarianship might be dangerous to the profession?*

Yes, I would say that. I think they are dangerous. But when I said it, I was speaking in terms of a particular situation and not making a generic statement. As I look at librarianship at the University of California, the aspiration is—and the important one it seems to me—for librarians to be participants with the teaching and research staff in the development of academic policy and planning. Now this means participatory administration. It means that members of the library staff, in a way similar to that of the teaching staff, are themselves governing themselves—are part of the governance of the university. If you move into the union style, then there is a gap between the employed and the employer. This is essential to the union point of view. The employer becomes involved in adversary tactics. You cannot be an adversary if you yourself are part of, really part of, the governance. This, I think, is the problem. And there has been a long tradition in the University of California, as good almost as in any university, a long tradition of the faculty governing the academic enterprise. The Academic Senate in the University of California is a very powerful and distinguished and effective body. The faculty could not think of themselves as employees of the University—it is just foreign to their whole attitude. If members of the library staff are to participate with those people, they have got to find a way of life which is of that kind. The union way, it seems to me, is another path. It would inhibit what many of us think is the best opportunity for librarians in this University now. Another university, another kind of institution, is another matter. I can see the importance of unions in a metropolitan public library, in a collegiate situation where the faculty are unionized, or where the style of the faculty is different. That's fine—I have no generic objection, but I think there is a difference in function here. If the library staff were pushed in the direction of unionization, they would shift away from being arm-in-arm with the faculty. This, I think, would be a dangerous change.

Earlier in our conversation, you used the word "participatory." The climate of the day seems to suggest that students should also participate in university governance or at least be involved as part of their educational experience. How do you think this can be accomplished in libraries?

Being the pragmatic person that I am, it is always hard for me to think theoretically and to separate myself from the local situation. But it just seems inescapable that academic institutions must somehow find a relevant adjustment with the aspirations of students today. Unless they find such an adjustment, the situation is going to be increasingly unhappy. In library terms, it seems to me terribly important that if there are student library committees they should be real and not just nominal library committees. Or, if there is a faculty library committee, that the students be represented on it in a real way with a voice, vote, and a method of appointment that makes them representative of the student group. They should have a real voice, in terms of service hours, circulation regulations, the development of collections in an undergraduate library, and so forth.

Do you see any advantage in having a separate student committee as contrasted to representation on the faculty library committee?

I could see a place for both depending upon how the institution operates. If the library committee of the faculty is a meaningless body, I would say develop a good student library committee. If the faculty library committee is an active body, the student representative can make a contribution, particularly over a period of time. I think this is all a kind of new experience with most of us and with most students. And you have to develop something in the way of a tradition or an esprit or ambience in which it becomes a creative experience and not just a student political move.

California has been a pioneer in many progressive library plans. What has been significant in the way of cooperative effort in this area?

It is sad to say but I don't really think that we have much to offer and I am disappointed to have to admit this. You would think that with all the wealth of the state and the forward-looking librarians who have been out here that some very fine things in the way of library cooperation would have taken place. I do not know of any major library idea or major library development in cooperation that has come from this part of the country. We have talked a good deal about it as everybody does, but so far it has been pretty much talk. For many years there was a wonderful, wonderful old man at Claremont College named Willis Kerr. He was librarian of the Claremont College group and perhaps in mentioning him I am suggesting the one creative act in academic library cooperation in this part of the country that I can think of offhand. Claremont Colleges, as you know, are a coordinated group of independently endowed collegiate institutions with a common graduate school and a common research library. The concept of a central research library was, I suppose, Willis Kerr's idea. At any rate he was there when it got started and built the first library. Willis was a man of great generosity of spirit and cordiality, and always supported any kind of cooperative enterprise that made sense. I am sure that developing a common library for a group of geographically but otherwise unrelated colleges was a creative act—a very important one. Aside from that, one would think that in the University of California—nine campuses, a single president, a single board of regents—that we would have designed something uncommon in the way of coordination. We have worked together in a common Library Council for some twenty-five years or more; but we haven't accomplished much. We have talked, kept in touch, avoided fragmentation and competition, I suppose, but we haven't done anything very creative in the way of cooperation.

Does this mean that library cooperation will not amount to much unless it involves institutional agreements to limit the scope of faculty teaching and research?

I think this one of the facts of life. We are just finishing the decade of the 1960's during which the University of California has been operating under a master plan of higher education. Involved in that was a library plan for the 1960's which made provisions for two major research libraries—Berkeley and UCLA. The new campuses would move up as fast as they could but call on the big, central research libraries for assistance. In that original discussion there was talk of specialization which is an old red herring in cooperative agreements. Clark Kerr, the president who instituted all this, was a very great man and a kind of martyr to the educational cause in this state. So it is hard to speak ill of him. But when he was first president he picked up a lot of symbolic library ideas. For example, the storage library—this was great stuff. Harvard had a storage library. Ergo storage libraries were good. There would be storage libraries. Specialization sounds like a good thing so we will specialize. Thus it was written in that the libraries wouldn't duplicate in their areas of excellence. UCLA had a Near Eastern studies institute so it would build up Near Eastern collections. Berkeley had a Far Eastern institute, so it would build up Far Eastern collections. Well, the dynamics of academic excellence are such that in my judgment a library cannot specialize unless its own faculty specializes in terms of teaching and research. When the Berkeley faculty starts teaching Near Eastern linguistics and the economics of the Middle East, they will have to buy Near Eastern books at Berkeley and it doesn't make a damn bit of difference to them that we have them at UCLA. They can't teach a seminar five hundred miles away making regular use of books down here, except for the unusual, occasional book that you borrow. So specialization falls apart, it seems to me, unless the institution has the determination to control the pattern of its academic activity, and maybe it is unrealistic to think that this can be done. If it can, then the library is in the clear and it can specialize. Unless the institutions specialize and formalize such agreements, the librarian is the fall guy. He'd get killed if he told his faculty *no* when they want to hire the best Near East economist from Harvard. He wants books. The librarian can't say no.

Is the Institute of Library Research a product of your Library Council?

Yes, there is one place where I think that we can take some pride in cooperation. Within the last five years it was our idea that given the size and wealth and potential of the University of California and the ambition of the libraries, it was about time that we got away from the concept of the working librarian doing research about library development. This is like the old-fashioned shipmaster navigating by his thumb and the stars. It seemed to us that we needed full-time academic brains devoted to research in the library area as importantly as full-time research brains are dedicated to agriculture or medicine or highway engineering. The library problems today seem to be equally important socially and equally complex intellectually. So, modeled on the concept of the Institute of Government and Public Affairs and the Institute of Geophysics, we thought of an interdisciplinary research center which would bring to bear the brains of anybody interested in any aspect of the library problem, whether physicist, engineer, economist, or specialist in public administration. This was set up as a university-wide organization but associated with the library schools so that it would have access to graduate students, research assistants, and provide thesis activities in these schools, while at the same time serving the ends of research in the library field. It is not an internal library operating department but an interdisciplinary research enterprise.

Was the idea readily accepted by the University?

It's very interesting. We first began talking with our faculties about this idea back in the early 1960's and they didn't know what we were talking about. They said, "Well, hire another clerk. You have a problem, so hire another librarian." They didn't see the intellectual problem. But then about the same time along came all this loose talk about information science, information transfer, and so forth. This began to ring a bell in the minds of some of the faculty, at least to the point where we captured a few of them, and they suddenly said, "Well, my goodness, this does sound exciting." Then federal research money became available. The National Science Foundation and Office of Education showed interest. This kind of helped change faculty minds, too. It took some doing, but now it is accepted and it is listed along with the Near Eastern Studies center, the Institute of Geophysics, and the Institute of Brain Research. It is a state-wide research institute and the director happens to be on the library school faculty at UCLA. The associate director is a member of the library school faculty at Berkeley.

Do you see any conflict between the scholarly aspects of librarianship as we have known them in the past and the current interest in automation and information? Someone has said that the latter "is not a trend; it has become a state of mind."

I don't think there is any real discrepancy between intellectual ambitions and the newer concepts of automation if they are looked at in the right terms. I think one thing that will happen is that we will be drawing bright youngsters into the library business from fields which we didn't tap before. We are getting bright young men and women from the graduate school of business, engineering, mathematics, and the sciences who see in the intellectual problems of information science—in the more abstruse sense of the term, not merely the technological—who see in this a field of excitement. I believe we will pull more and more people who are capable of systems design and development into the library business for its own good. These are people who in many instances might have become mathematicians or systems engineers. I think we will have a richer pool of brains in the library field in the future than we now have.

You believe then that we can bring this new technology under the umbrella of librarianship?

I think this is most important. One of the things we have been pleased with here is that the library school has been receptive to teaching information science and doing research in it and has not left it to the school of engineering. It is an aspect of librarianship. If at the same time we do not forget the bibliographical side, then I would hope, as you suggest, that it will fall into place. I do not think we should be training programmers. Librarians should handle the implications of this whole new world, control it, and shape it.

Ruth Walling

RUTH WALLING is one of the outstanding women librarians in the United States. She was born in Dallas, Texas; graduated from Southern Methodist and Texas College for Women (B.A., 1931; and B.A. in L.S., 1935), and some six years later received an M.A. from the Graduate Library School of the University of Chicago.

In 1964 Miss Walling received the Isadore Gilbert Mudge Citation from the Reference Services Division of the ALA from which is quoted, with deletion and without permission, the following:

for: "her constructive work in developing the reference collections and services of three academic libraries, East Texas State College, Louisiana State University, and Emory University, her excellence as a reference librarian . . . , gift for communication, and an empathy for readers at all levels . . . , her selfless generosity in helping colleagues, and her rich sense of humor which illuminates all her relations with others."

The following year she received the Savannah (Georgia) State College Library award with the following citation:

for: "the quiet, steadfast, and overwhelmingly effective role she played, both locally and nationally, in the successful drive toward the racial integration of the American Library Association and its affiliated chapters."

Certainly there is a greatness in this librarian—something which puts her in a class by herself. Of the impact and distinction she makes, even on first meeting, one may use the word "personality," but her personality is compounded of many qualities beyond those of generosity, humor, and humanity which are cited in the two awards mentioned above. What these qualities are is a very difficult thing for an average writer to express, but most certainly they include the qualities of sincerity, integrity, and genuine goodwill.

The interview took place July 21, 1969, in Atlanta, where Miss Walling serves as Associate University Librarian, Emory University.

Reference work is a vague and inadequate phrase to describe what reference librarians do. C. C. McCombs, a distinguished bibliographer, once said that it is "help given by the librarian to a reader in finding books or facts needed for some sort of particular purpose." Does that describe the fundamental character of reference work in the university library?

I think it does. My own working definition, possibly just a restatement, is that reference work is making materials available to users to meet a specific need. Any of the activities commonly carried out by the reference department of a university library are directed toward this end, whether it's determining where certain information may be found, conducting a literature search, selecting several good books on a subject, verifying a reference, compiling a bibliography, assisting in the use of the card catalog, providing access to material not in the card catalog, borrowing a book on interlibrary loan, obtaining a photocopy of a manuscript, locating a periodical in another library, arranging for the use of outside resources and bibliographical services—the list could go on almost endlessly. Even the teaching function, such an important part of university reference, comes within the definition, but adds another dimension.

Do you distinguish in reference between factual and research questions?

Reference departments often attempt to make a distinction in recording statistics, although we do not. The distinction will vary in different libraries. It may be based on the length of time required to answer the question. It may be based on the number of sources used. A fact question is supposed to require less time and fewer sources than a research question. Neither of these distinctions is valid. One might bring to bear a number of sources to establish a simple fact, such as a birth date, if there is disagreement among the sources. One may spend hours tracking down an elusive quotation. But a fact question has one answer, and once this is found and judged to be correct, the question is completely handled. Not so the research question, which is typically a request for information on a subject, and for which there is no single answer. The materials sought out to meet the request are usually determined by the purpose of the request and the level of sophistication of the inquirer. Or the subject may be an obscure one which requires the piecing together of bits of information from scattered and sometimes unlikely sources.

Miss Isadore Mudge of Columbia used to say that the card catalog is the most useful of all reference tools. Is this true today?

I would say that it is still the single most important one but there are factors which diminish its usefulness for reference in relation to other reference tools. In Miss Mudge's day I would guess the Columbia card catalog contained full cataloging, including analytics, for everything owned by the library. This would probably not be true of any university library today. There are large microfilm and microfiche projects which are whole libraries in themselves and which may not be in the card catalog. United States government documents are not most efficiently approached through the card catalog even when they are there, but rather through their own indexes. Also, there is some evidence that subject cards are now less used than author cards. This seems an inevitable result of the proliferation of cards under a subject, the rapid obsolescence of many subject headings, and various inconsistencies resulting from tinkering with them. For many questions, I do not start with the card catalog. Sometimes I should have because I have gone all the way around the barn and the answer is right there in the card catalog. Usually one thinks in terms of identifying first what the best sources will be, and then using the card catalog as a finding tool. I think this is particularly true in a field about which one knows very little, or if the subject is broad. Five minutes spent with the bibliography at the end of the article on the "Philosophy of Education" in the *Encyclopedia of Philosophy* is worth an hour at the card catalog.

Is it possible that in the future, particularly if libraries turn more and more to machine generated catalogs, that the card catalog will become less a reference tool and more simply a locating tool?

This is a very real possibility. Actually, the card catalog itself is not as accurate bibliographically as in Miss Mudge's day. To cite one instance. for many of the reprints, which are now so numerous, Library of Congress cataloging does not give the date of the original edition. If the library owns the reprint of the second edition of Cordier's *Bibliotheca Sinica*, for example, the unwitting card catalog user, judging from the 1966 imprint that here is an up-to-date bibliography of China, is apt to be disappointed when he finds it was first published in 1904.

You mentioned a minute ago that identifying the best source usually precedes going to the catalog. Is the identification of the best source the first step in handling a reference question?

I think that I should regard the first step as finding out exactly what the reader wants, what he is asking for, and why he is asking for it. One needs to know *why* because it is part of defining the question and deciding on how much material the reader is going to need, what kind, and in what form. Recently a faculty member asked where the anthropologists were listed. Three other people were waiting, so he was hastily shown *American Men of Science*. Later we followed up. The anthropologist was nineteenth century and the faculty member was not interested in the man himself, but only in certain events of his early life as they affected his sister, the real subject of research. Obviously nothing short of a full scale biography would do, and this has not been written. The answer may lie in the anthropologist's papers, which we were able to locate in another library.

Which is most important in reference work, to know books or to have a good general background of knowledge?

Each is indispensable, but if a person has a good general background of knowledge, he can perhaps acquire a knowledge of books. I assume you are thinking here particularly of reference books. I don't know how an impoverished cultural background can be remedied. In every Gallup poll, you know, there are always 20 percent of the people who never heard of the subject. They would never make good reference librarians, and yet they turn up sometimes on reference staffs.

Does one have to be a totally dedicated person to be a good reference librarian?

I'm just sitting here trying to think of the good reference librarians I have known and whether I would call them dedicated or not. I suppose it depends on what you mean by dedicated. I do not think a nine to five person can be a good reference librarian. There is just too much to know and too much to read. One advantage the reference librarian has over other persons who must read every waking hour to keep up in their fields is that he can range far and wide in his reading. Literally nothing he knows is wasted. But the most helpful reading for me are books which show how scholars work (footnotes can be the most important part), surveys of subject fields, and dealers' catalogs. A real reference librarian will be dedicated in another sense. He will not be entirely happy if he has to give up without finding whatever the reader may have asked about. Many times I have observed reference librarians who have devoted a great deal of time to a complex or obscure problem, but are still not getting anywhere with it. They have gone through all the logical steps and have covered everything one can reasonably expect them to cover. They have probably spent more time on it than they should, and it looks hopeless. It is at this point that the dedicated (and perhaps inspired) reference librarian will begin all over again with a fresh approach, and worry along with it until the solution is found.

When I attended library school the theory was that since a reference librarian's job was to answer questions, the student's job was to learn the books thoroughly which had all the answers. Is this possible today when so many hundreds of new reference books appear each year?

No, it is not possible by the traditional method of studying the content and arrangement of each book. While any examination helps, thorough knowledge may have to be gained by use. The best method for gaining a practical working knowledge of the collection seems to be to categorize in one's mind individual titles by subject and type and remember them that way. For philosophy, for example, Lester Asheim in *The Humanities and the Library*, lists reference works under "dictionaries and encyclopedias," "bibliographies," "biographical tools," and "reference histories" as the essential types for that particular field. I believe problems used in reference courses now tend to follow this pattern.

Was this method of studying reference books first introduced by Dean H. S. Hirshberg of Western Reserve?

I do not know, but the work that carries out the method beautifully is Carl White's *Sources of Information in the Social Sciences*. I think it is the best book of its kind. After a discussion of the nature and history of each of the social sciences and a listing of landmark books, the basic reference and bibliographic works in the field are listed by type, and annotated.

At a Chicago Institute I once attended, John W. Spargo, an English scholar, said something similar to what you have just said about knowing reference books through using them constantly. But if I recall correctly, he spoke somewhat disparagingly about the reference librarian's training. I believe he thought that the reference librarian would be far better off studying and doing research in a particular field than in conning titles in Mudge. I don't suppose many reference librarians would agree with this?

I don't believe that I do. I think it would help to the extent of knowing what is involved in research—afford a better understanding of that—but for taking care of the very miscellaneous questions that come up every day, I doubt that it would. If such a person were to superimpose a field of specialization on top of a thorough knowledge of bibliography in the areas in which he is going to do reference work, then that would be fine. I think that primarily reference librarians need to be specialists in bibliography. I think it is possible to accomplish this even in many fields, and that it is most important. Any good reference librarian has a chance of knowing more about the bibliography of a subject than the people who are working in the field themselves, who all too often are not experts in their own bibliography. It is good, however, to have the staff even in general reference trained in different subject fields. A question may come to any member of the staff, but it will be referred to the one who is most competent to handle it.

University libraries cannot hope to attain the universality of collections which their title denotes. Yet I have been told this is a desirable goal in building the reference collection. What do you think?

I would agree that it is. You might hesitate to buy very much in an area that is not represented in the curriculum or research program of the university, but the reference collection must enable faculty and students to do pre-research over the array of knowledge and scholarship. It seems to me that the range of subjects should approach universality and that the bibliographical coverage should be as broad and comprehensive as possible. Here is a simple example. One likes to think if an item has ever appeared in print, there is a good chance of identifying it through the bibliography available in the reference collection.

Are there many reference or research questions where it is necessary to turn to reference material outside the fields of university instruction and research?

Yes, I certainly think so, particularly for students who are writing theses and dissertations. It is very difficult to predict the ramifications of a subject and where they are going to lead. Our university offers no work in agriculture, but the early years of the *Agricultural Index* have been used by the social historians. Of course the reference collection will reflect the curriculum and research interests of the university by its strengths and weaknesses. We will not have a strong reference collection in agriculture, but we will have the basic titles. I am somewhat less certain about whether the reference collection should be limited by language. Should reference works in a language read by very few people be acquired? No one presently at this university reads the Czech language, and we buy few or no publications from Czechoslovakia. Should the reference collection have the leading Czech encyclopedia, which happens to be an outstanding one? Should we acquire the sets making up the national bibliography of Czechoslovakia? For many large university libraries this would not be a good illustration. They would think it strange that one would raise the question.

Even with universality as a goal, are there not practical limiting factors?

Yes, space and cost. Modern technologies—the reprint industry, photocopying processes, and the computer—have made reference works available that the reference librarian formerly would have considered the wildest of dreams. But costs to the libraries are astronomical, and there is too much duplication. Two projects for computer-produced concordances to Shakespeare's works are now in progress. A computerized index to literature on oceanography was begun three or four years ago, although two or three other current indexing services on the subject were already being published. Perhaps another was needed, but when several hundred dollars a year are involved, one is going to investigate very carefully. However, duplication is not the major problem. There are a great many major sets and services that are obviously worthwhile, but since funds are not unlimited, difficult choices must be made.

I am sure there are numerous approaches and techniques in building a reference collection. One that intrigues me is the idea of "building on failure." The phrase may have been Miss Mudge's. Do reference librarians make any systematic attempt to secure titles which might have provided the answers if they had been available in the collection when the request was made?

Yes, very often gaps are discovered in this way, not only in reference holdings, but in other parts of the collections, and titles are added as a result. Probably this "building on failure" is not as systematic as it should be, at times when the staff is working under pressure, with no moments to pick up pieces in between requests. The idea is built into the selection process, however, and whether we are conscious of it or not is always a factor in considering titles for purchase. It becomes a very conscious process when we are continually looking for works that will assist in handling questions that recur.

Would there be any virtue in having a clearinghouse of

194 *The Librarian Speaking*

unanswered questions to point up the availability of books which supply the answers?

It would be worth trying, but would take a lot of doing. The danger would be that the clearinghouse would turn out to be a collection of odd facts which will be found in unexepected places, and of obscure questions which are found, if at all, by serendipity, or by some specialist who happens to know. At the other extreme would be the danger that the books that supplied the answers were already familiar to reference librarians. Neither would assist in book selection. There is an area in between. Right now I should like to know if there is a work which identifies banners carried into battle as belonging to a particular person at a specific date for European countries during the fifteenth and sixteenth centuries.

A substantial portion of the annual funds needed for maintaining a reference collection goes for serials. How do you go about selecting serials for reference purposes? There are no reviews, or very few if any, I believe. ESP?

Perhaps, in part. And I wouldn't say there aren't mistakes made. The cost is a continuing one, and many are very expensive. So it is a very real problem, and you are right in saying that reviews seldom appear. Many of these serials first come to one's attention through publishers' brochures. If one is sufficiently on guard, there is a great deal to be learned from them. An experienced reference librarian knows when the brochure first hits his desk whether or not the publication will fill a real need. For example, a year or so ago an announcement was received about a new index to philosophy journals. Philosophy happens to be a subject well covered by its indexing services. A check of the journals the new index proposed to examine confirmed that the new index would not broaden coverage. There remained questions of currency and access, of course. If the serial is a needed service, then publisher, sponsorship, and other factors can be studied. There are projects that are obviously being undertaken with insufficient staff and resources, usually doomed to be short lived. Not every decision is this easy, however. One troublesome type for me is publications devoted to listing current contents of periodicals in a field. They have found a place in the sciences, and are now invading the social sciences. How much are we justified in investing in services which are convenient but which add nothing to the permanent bibliographical resources? In general, however, if the new service is a bibliographical tool and if it seems likely to add any coverage at all, one is disposed toward adding it if possible.

Does the scholar make a contribution to building a reference collection?

Yes, most certainly. He sometimes calls attention to a new work which might otherwise be missed. He may even be a contributor to it and gives the reference department advance notice about it. Whether he is a contributor or not, he will know the scholars who are. Most important, he will know how the title fits into his field, and whether it is relevant to the teaching and research program of his department. An even more valuable contribution can be made by the scholar who calls attention to gaps in his subject in the reference collection. Still another way he may contribute is with advice on titles which the reference librarian thinks should be considered but is uncertain about because of lack of knowledge of the field.

Is there any reason to be on your guard regarding the scholar's recommendations?

He may ride his specialization and seek costly specialized works at the expense of more widely used reference tools. Or, since relatively few faculty members will be active in recommending titles, the collection could become unbalanced. There will even be instances when the recommended title is either of no value *per se*, or of no value to that particular library.

In the January, 1964, Library Trends *Margaret Goggin and Lillian Seaberg state that "the reviewing of reference books is highly inadequate as far as their existence and the rapidity of their appearance are concerned." How do you go about locating reviews of particular reference books and how do you reach a decision as to purchase if no reviews are available?*

The statement is as true today as it was five years ago, particularly for foreign titles. There are a great many publications which review some reference books, but we have nothing which is systematically covering them. For currently published reference books, I rarely take the time to look for a review of a particular reference book. Rather, I regularly go through all the media which review them, plus some scholarly journals. I have already mentioned some of the other ways I try to find out about a title. Still others are on intuition backed up only by knowledge of the author, publisher, or need for the subject. Your ESP again.

How about College and Research Libraries? *Is it helpful for reviews of reference books?*

I suppose you refer to the semi-annual series now edited by Eugene Sheehy. Yes, it is the nearest thing to systematic coverage which we have, although not comprehensive. The notes are descriptions rather than reviews, but they are usually full enough to enable one to determine whether the title will be useful in the reference collection. For most of the titles we have already made our decision before the list comes out, but never fail to pick up some that we did not know of. *Choice* is making a contribution for reference works published in the United States. There are many other guides; they all contribute a little, but each is inadequate.

Is there a place for a reviewing media devoted entirely to reference literature?

I think there is a need for a journal which reviews reference books and reviews them promptly enough to make a difference.

Since reference books are so very expensive and growing more so is there anything which libraries in a particular area can do to share resources?

I think that for bibliography, reference, and pre-research the library needs the materials in its own library. We expect to go outside for the books after readers find out what they want, but the reference works are needed to identify what they want.

A large university library is not easy to use. I know that reference librarians have worked tirelessly over the years to provide some sort of class instruction in the fundamentals of library use, often without too great a success. You have had a great deal of experience with this and have a new program ready to start this fall. Can you tell us something about it?

The program represents some advance beyond our previous instruction in the use of the library because it will be extended to the junior class. For several years we have had two library lectures in one of the required English courses for freshmen, but regularly scheduled library instruction ended there. Beginning this fall, the program for freshmen has been revised, and two lectures will be inaugurated for juniors. This is still very little time, but is as much as is feasible and practical. We plan to use it to make the students aware of resources that are available for them, to introduce them to procedures for identifying and locating these resources, and to give them some guidance as to how they can go ahead and discover other things for themselves. We are concerned that students need very badly what the library has to offer and often express shock and surprise when they discover too late that it exists.

The freshmen will have two lectures which meet the same week in the fall quarter. These will be given in classes of approximately forty students each. The lectures are being called "Introduction to Library Resources." The first lecture will cover the services which the university and undergraduate libraries have to offer; we plan to use slides in this presentation. The second lecture will discuss the card catalog and the periodical indexes and again we shall use slides to show what can be done with the card catalog and the periodical indexes. In this second lecture we shall also talk about a few very basic reference books. We shall give the students an annotated list of reference books selected as basic to undergraduate studies. These lectures will be given in the library, where a special room is provided for the purpose. Some of the books will be brought into the library room; in fact we shall be able to do just about anything we want so far as illustrative material is concerned.

You mentioned that the instruction would be extended to juniors. When and how does this get underway?

Also in the fall quarter. When the student reaches the end of the sophomore year, he selects a major. We think this is the best time to follow up with the next phase of library instruction. It is the level at which the student becomes more involved in independent use of the library, writes more term papers, and the like. There will be a series of three two-hour lectures called "Library Resources and Research Techniques," one series in the humanities, one in the social sciences, and one in mathematics and the natural sciences. These correspond to the formal college divisions, and all majors fall into one of the three divisions. Our meetings will be conducted as seminars in a conference room which is a part of the reference office suite. Each seminar will have a maximum of fourteen students. The leader of the seminar will be drawn from members of the library reference staff who specialize in the respective areas. There will be two seminar meetings for each group. The limited time presents a real problem in the selection of material because of the breadth of the divisions. For example, instruction would include the general works which should be common knowledge, then there are works which include all of the social sciences or all of the humanities.

Beyond these, we need to introduce the students to at least a few basic titles in the specific subject fields. I think this can best be done by using them as illustrations of types of bibliographical aids—as *International Bibliography of Political Science* for current bibliography, *Current Sociology* for reviews of the literature, *Historical Abstracts* for abstracting services, etc. To accompany these seminars there will be rather extensive mimeographed lists of selected bibliographies and reference works in the three areas.

Perhaps you will be able to recreate something of the excitement which a library school student feels when he takes his first reference course?

I hope so, but we must avoid entirely any approach of a professional library instruction nature and try to get to the student from the standpoint of the particular problems he has to solve. What we want to do is to begin with the problem and not particular books, the problem which the student has to work out in a library and to suggest the kinds of materials that are there to assist him.

Is this course, lectures, seminar, call it what you will, a part of an English course?

No, it has been worked out with the Office of the Dean of the College, which has approved the lectures and set up the machinery for sectioning the students and getting them to the lectures. For the junior lectures, if they are to flourish, we will need to enlist what we hope will be the enthusiastic support of the faculty. A great deal depends upon how well received by the students the seminars are at the beginning. Looking beyond the seminars based on the three broad divisions of the curriculum, we are hoping they will generate interest for more specialized instruction in sections on history, political science, and other subject fields.

Experienced reference librarians should be in an excellent position to prepare guides to sources of information. What do you think about these as an aid to students in the use of the library?

We have relied quite heavily upon guides to try to educate students and faculty about services and resources. We have a leaflet series which includes guides to sources in romance languages, education, biology, chemistry, and government documents. In two or three of these, we tried to combine the basic tools, annotated, with suggestions as to how to go about literature searches. I cannot say how effective these guides are; I don't think we know. We have had a certain amount of interest shown by people who have received them. It varies, and it is not an interest that will continue if it is not prodded now and then. We brought out a biology leaflet and distributed it to the faculty in the field, saying that copies would be available for distribution to their classes. The first time there were not enough copies to meet the requests. It was revised, brought out again in the same way, and it was not in as much demand as formerly. This might be taken as an indication that the faculty didn't find it particularly useful. I do not know how else to interpret it. The experience with the romance language leaflet was quite different. The department invited the Reference Department to take part in a seminar they were holding for all their graduate students. It was a seminar which met about five times and dealt with various aspects of research and two hours were devoted to the bibliography of the romance languages. We worked out the leaflet for the specific purpose of using it in these seminars and it has been very well received.

Have recent developments in machine technology as applied to libraries had any effect on reference materials and services?

So far the principal effect has been to produce many bibliographies and reference works which would not have appeared at all without the computer. *Science Citation Index* is an obvious example. Computer-produced concordances are opening up new possibilities in textual criticism for scholars in the various literatures. Other indexes have been speeded up. The subject index for *Biological Abstracts* used to appear about three years late, and now appears monthly. We should be thankful for this, I'm sure, and not quibble about not being able to retrieve every article on a subject by means of a key-word-in-context index.

Enough abstracting and indexing services are now working toward putting their indexing on tapes for computer searching to indicate the condition of the future. We already have Medlars, Datrix, and various other services, and *Chemical Abstracts* is moving ahead. What is difficult for me to predict is what the effect on the reference department as we know it today will be. So far the effect has been that we have a growing number of new services which we must keep up with and inform our users about whenever appropriate—again in the interest of making material available. We have not experienced as yet any upsurge of use of these services by our readers. Another effect has been the rise in cost of computer-produced indexes. The increase has been so great that one wonders if libraries are going to be able to afford them.

Before closing this interview I should like to ask you two or three questions about what librarianship is really all about— reading itself. You are the most discriminating reader I know personally. You have a sensitivity of perception and an independent literary judgment which I find rare among the librarians whom I know well. How does one develop such qualities?

That's a tremendously difficult question to answer. First, it is necessary to thank you for the compliment, but demur that it may not be so. Second, even if it were, I have no idea how discrimination in reading would be developed. If I say that reading has always been like breathing to me, it sounds trite, but it is true. I became interested in libraries from reading in my neighborhood branch library when I was very young. I read for the sheer enjoyment of it, read everything that was there without discrimination. Maybe there's a Gresham's Law of reading that works in reverse. Perhaps my library school instruction helped the process along.

In what way?

There was a conscious effort made by a research-oriented faculty to develop a critical attitude toward glittering generalities and dogmatic statements not backed up by research. Many of the articles we read were not to learn anything about the content, but to tear them apart and criticize them.

For a number of years you have met regularly with a small number of librarians to discuss books and book reviews. Does this kind of teamwork, attentive and questioning review study in a systematic and continuous way, have anything to do with making a critical book reader?

Yes, I should have mentioned this experience before. You, being the originator of the idea, know that we operated under rather rigorous ground rules. Each member of the group was reading regularly two or three general reviewing media and covering reviews in some twenty-five scholarly periodicals. We were trying to select significant general books which did not fall within the responsibility of the academic departments, and our recommendations were usually based on several reviews of a particular title. It was necessary to learn enough about the book from the reviews to give the other members of the group a clear idea of its content, purpose, style, competence of the author, sources, authority, strengths and weaknesses, contribution to the literature of the subject. One also had to be prepared to answer rather probing questions from the others. Under these circumstances every word in a review is going to be read and weighed. It was a revelation to find that often some of these fundamentals could not be answered even from several reviews. The reviews in the scholarly journals, with a few honorable exceptions, do not stand up better in this regard than do those in the general reviewing media.

I believe the meetings were beneficial in making more critical book readers of us. From our own reading of reviews and from the presentations of others in the group, we knew a great deal about the books we were selecting, and various ones of us probably read books we would not have otherwise been interested in. We frequently had occasion in our meetings to mention our opinions of these books.

There are in general two main sources of reviews, the regular reviewing media and the scholarly and professional journals. What is your opinion regarding the state of reviewing in the weekly book review journals?

For a long time I thought the *New York Times Book Review* was the best of the general reviews simply because of its coverage and promptness and because I thought the reviews told what the book was about. I know that it has been said that the reviews treat books as news, not critically, but for a period of several years the lead reviews were written by scholars in the field, whose judgment was usually later confirmed by the reviews in the scholarly journals. My impression is that the *New York Times Book Review* is not now providing as comprehensive coverage of the new books, and that the quality of the reviews has not been maintained.

The *New York Review* contains delightful essays but the reviews are devoted to the ideas of the reviewer which may or may not have anything to do with the book under review. Their reviews infuriate me for this reason, and I think the *Times Literary Supplement*, guilty of the same thing from away back, is getting more this way than ever before. Too many of its reviews provide essays on the subject of the book, but say nothing about the book. I used to like the *Saturday Review* but I haven't been reading it lately. I think the computer lost my subscription. But as you know it no longer contains a large number of reviews since the *Review* became a general periodical rather than a book-reviewing journal.

Are there other weeklies which you would put high on your list; if so for what particular qualities?

For many years I have read each week the book review section of *The Nation*, and with slightly less regularity, of the *New Republic*. Each reviews relatively few books. For this reason, perhaps, the titles reviewed are apt to be important, and among them, over a period of time, will be a few not widely reviewed elsewhere. *Nation* reviews are long, in depth, and often have originality and insights not commonly found in book reviews. Some of the same values are provided by the English weeklies, the *New Statesman* and the *Spectator*, although one wishes the *Spectator* would like a book now and then.

One limitation of the weeklies is that they duplicate their reviews so much that only a small percentage of the important books are covered. Do the professional and scholarly journals extend the range? I'm thinking of general, scholarly books rather than those on abstruse and recondite subjects.

Of course the professional and scholarly journals extend the range, but the state of coverage appears to be chaotic. Only a handful of the scholarly journals seem to be methodically reviewing the books which are being published in their fields. Some give valuable space to reviews of books not in their fields. One suspects that all too many are selecting from among whatever review copies happen to be sent to them. Many times in the reference department, in assisting library users to find reviews, we fail to locate any through the indexes to reviews, even for titles that have been out for several years. Which brings me to my other complaint against the scholarly journals—the length of time that often elapses between publication of the book and appearance of the review. For some journals three years is about average, and we have learned to expect to wait at least a year for the scholarly reviews. For book selection in a library this deliberateness makes the scholarly journals, which should be the most helpful of all aids as the most authoritative, probably the least useful.

Index